A Portrait of
BASILDON PLOTLANDS

The Enduring Spirit

A Portrait of
BASILDON PLOTLANDS

The Enduring Spirit

DEANNA WALKER
and
PETER JACKSON

Phillimore

2010

Published by
PHILLIMORE & CO. LTD
Healey House, Andover, Hampshire

ISBN 978 1 86077 622 9

Manufacturing managed by
Jellyfish Print Solutions Ltd

Contents

Acknowledgements and Thanks

Deanna – A big thanks to Paul for all his help, and especially for listening to my incessant chatter about the plotlands. You've been a good boy!

I'd like to make a dedication to my mum, whose laughter I will always miss and whose diaries inspired me to write this book.
For Gladys Darwin, 1924-2009.

Peter – Many thanks to Helen for her patience and for reading through the drafts sympathetically.

*   *   *

We would like to offer our sincere thanks to the following people for their contributions, advice or interest in this project. Apologies to anyone we have inadvertently missed!

Marion Allwood, Dave and Jean Anderson, Jean and Arthur Anderson, Michael Anthony, Jessie and Bill Armitage, Ron Ashton, Harry Bacon, Maud and Charles Barry and Catherine Stack, Marian Berry, Eric and Florence Biggs and Tina Winwood, David Blaine, Betty Brown, Joe Bruce, Maureen Buck, Alan Burton, Dennis Burton, Joyce Burton, Chris Bytheway, Audrey Carter (and a special thanks for helping to rally the contributions of former plotlanders who attend her reunions), Rod Cole, Hilda Collier, Rose Cousins, Ron and Georgie Crafer, Jean Dallinger, Jean Darby, Alan Davies, Carole Devlin, Jean and Henry Dickinson, Lesley Elliot, Peter Ellis, Ray Ellis, Gladys Fenn, Phylis Frasi and her sister Dorothy, Karen Garner, Joe Goodman, Denise Hamilton, Vera Harris, Elsie Hill, Mr Howard, Colin Humphrey, Pat Jackson, Wallace Jackson, Sue Jenkins and her sister Pauline, Ivy King, Roy King, Clive Layton, Don Liddiard, Emily McManus, Mark McManus, Brian Mills, Janet Morey, Sheila Mountfort, Jean Newberry, Ken Page, Sylvia Poole, Ken Porter, Ron Powell, David Richards, Ken Rowden, Denise Rowling, Karen Sebers (for her past contributions to the Dunton Plotland website), Betty Smith, Valerie Stocker,

Nick Street, Jeanne Sussex, Joan Tivendale and Phyl Kennerly, Gill Trerise, Diane and David Tyson, Tom and Anne Wallace, Linda Wilks, Sylvia Wright.

To the staff and volunteers at the Essex Wildlife Trust Langdon Reserve, in particular: Sue Adams, Maria Donohue, Karen McKay and Norman Allen (for his hot cross buns and coffee. We wouldn't have survived our 'scanning' event without him!). To Mick Coulson of the Land Restoration Trust's Langdon Lake and Meadow site.

To Ruth Costello and all the staff at Essex Records Office.

To all the staff at Phillimore publishers.

In particular, we'd like to thank Nina Humphrey for her enthusiasm and energy, and for contributing so many memories to this book. It's been a pleasure getting to know her. Nina would like to dedicate her writing as follows:

> For my brother, Dennis, who passed away recently, and for my
> late nephew, Paul Burton,whose warm, friendly and cheerful
> personality was so much a part of my childhood. He shared
> my love of the countryside around 'Spion Kop', always lending
> a helping hand whenever needed and keeping us laughing
> while getting the hay in. I love and miss you both.

Peter Jackson outside 'Vera-Joan'
in Hillcrest Aveune, *c.*1954.

Introduction

A scrubland full of ghosts,
And memories of happier times.
(Mark McManus)

This was how a young resident of Basildon described the plotland landscape in the mid-1980s when he discovered the few remaining huts and bungalows in the final days before their destruction. He recognised instantly that he was witnessing the passing of something unique. Although the land has now been redeveloped, a strong sense of the former plotland spirit still endures.

When I wrote *Basildon Plotlands* in 2001 I wanted to share tales from weekenders who owned plots in the countryside. After all, that was my experience of plotland life, as my parents owned a hut from 1954-83. However, in the last decade I have had the pleasure of meeting a number of Laindon's and Dunton's permanent plotland residents, many of whom lived in the area from the 1930s. Some still live close by, others have moved away to other parts of Britain – or even as far away as Australia and New Zealand. Wherever they now find themselves, they all share the same passion and interest in their vanished community. In this book we will hear some of their stories.

My co-writer Peter Jackson's family is among them. His maternal and paternal grandparents owned neighbouring plots on the Dunton Hills Estate, which is how his parents met. He has vivid childhood memories of the plotlands, particularly as he used to make deliveries for a local shop on a trade bike. Some residents might even remember him earnestly pedalling up the steep hills in the 1960s.

In the first part of our book we will paint a portrait of the plotland estates near Laindon and Dunton from the 1920s-80s, and explain where they were located in relation to the area today. Using maps, photographs, a detailed survey of the area in 1949-50, diary entries and memories of former residents, we show the plotlanders' homes and give a flavour of their lives. We will even take a couple of whimsical walking tours based on memories from the 1950s and 1960s.

Life was not simply an endless round of sunny afternoon picnics and rambles to pick blackberries, so we will also look at the challenges the permanent residents faced, not least during the Second World War. Many of the residents shared similar origins, being Londoners who had bought their weekend plots before the war. During the Blitz their families escaped to the comparative safety of the countryside, settling permanently in the plotlands. However, as Peter shows in our chapter about the war, Dunton was not the totally safe environment they had hoped for.

In the second part of the book we will look at the decline and eventual destruction of the plotlands. With the establishment of Basildon as a New Town in 1949, the plotlanders' days were numbered. We shall see how Basildon Development Corporation set about its task of turning the untamed plotland frontier into a modern town, and what this meant for the residents. Finally, we shall hear more of Mark McManus's moving account of the last days of the little plotland homes.

You may be reading this introduction and wondering what on earth 'plotlands' and 'plotlanders' are – thinking you have stumbled across some kind of strange secret society. Let me briefly explain. In the late 19th and early 20th centuries, much of the farmland around Basildon fell out of use due to an agricultural depression. Farms could not be sold as going concerns, so they were divided up into small

A well being built at 'Peacehaven' in Ronald Avenue, *c*.1940s.

plots (normally around 20 feet by 140 feet) and sold by land agents. Sometimes auctions were held on the site, which often involved alcohol to loosen prospective buyers' wallets. The Fenchurch Street to Southend railway line gave easy access to the countryside in the days before car ownership was common, and often the railway company would supply a free train ticket to auction-goers. Plots tended to be bought by working-class Londoners who were looking for a chance to own a little piece of land on which they could erect a small hut or bungalow. This would become a base for weekend and holiday use, where families could gather to experience life in the countryside. Some made it their permanent home.

Typically, the roads were unmade and impassable in winter to motor vehicles. There were limited mains services or, in some locations, none at all. Water often came from wells, or from standpipes which were dotted around the area. A bucket in the shed served as the toilet, and the contents were emptied into a pit in the garden.

The history of the plotlands has generated a great deal of popular interest in the form of successive publications, events and reunions. The area remains a continuing source of fascination, even for generations

Arthur Vance enjoying a typical afternoon in the plotlands.

who have no direct memory of what the plotlands represented. 'The Haven', a former plotland bungalow owned by the Mills family, has been preserved as a museum on Essex Wildlife Trust's Langdon Nature Reserve and it provides an excellent educational resource. Traces of the past and the remains of buildings can still be found in the undergrowth on many parts of the reserve.

The spirit of the plotlands continues to live on beneath the urban sprawl of Basildon New Town. No matter what visions the planners might create for Basildon, or the 'Thames Gateway' region, we suspect the plotland spirit is bound to haunt the area for many years yet.

So let us now evoke this spirit as we lead you through the 'scrubland full of ghosts and memories of happier times' …

PART ONE

A PORTRAIT OF THE PLOTLANDS

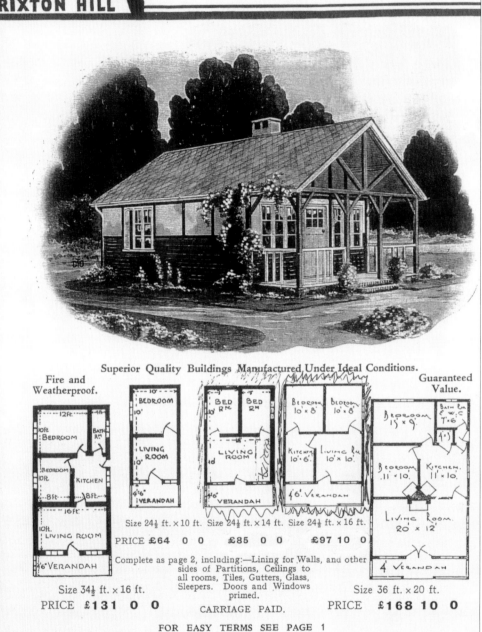

Kit used to build
'Eleanor' in
the 1930s.

Chapter 1

Plotland Architecture

Plotland communities with their unconventional architecture certainly polarised opinions. One man's beautiful wooden dwelling with a corrugated iron roof and a railway carriage cunningly attached to the side was another man's eyesore and blot on the landscape.

Until planning legislation in the 1940s stopped their spread, plotland developments had been springing up in a number of locations, such as along the east and south coasts and along the upper reaches of the River Thames. However, Essex had the largest concentration of plotland communities, including Canvey Island, Jaywick Sands, Havering Park and, of course, Pitsea, Billericay and Laindon.

Where entrepreneurs were responsible for the development of an estate and had a clear vision of what it should look like, as was the case with Jaywick Sands, they could help shape the overall layout and design of properties. Where land developers were simply dividing up the land into plots and selling them by auction, they were not so involved in what the owners were subsequently going to build. Restrictive covenants would be put in place to try to ensure that only buildings of a certain quality were erected, but in the interwar years it appears that building regulations were not strictly applied in all areas.

Many plotland homes were not supposed to be lived in permanently, and there are examples of owners being prosecuted if they were caught staying overnight in properties. However, it would have been an impossible task for council officials to prosecute all 'guilty parties' so only the unlucky were caught. Betty Brown's parents were unfortunately among them.

> We used to own a plotland shack in Billericay in the 1930s but my parents were prosecuted for sleeping in it. They were given a fine, and they were so incensed that they sold the plot and purchased another in the Laindon plotlands.

Plotland dwellings often started out as tents which were then replaced by very basic wooden properties, often designed and built entirely by the owners. However, once they had been extended several times and gone through multiple changes of cladding they could be transformed into quite desirable abodes. My dad clad our hut ('Halliford') with shiplap timber, but permanent dwellings would often be rendered with stucco or pebble-dash.

Nina Humphrey, whose family owned 'Spion Kop' in Laindon, said that she is still amazed by what her father, George Burton, was able to achieve single-handedly:

> He completely rebuilt the bungalow over the years. He changed the shape of the roof and gave it a higher pitch and moved the chimney from the corner of the building into the middle of the bungalow. I took it all for granted when I was a child as he was always doing something. There wasn't anything he wouldn't attempt.

Weekenders would get supplies delivered by local builders, or bring materials down (usually by train) from London. Normally

The house that Jack built. Charles 'Jack' Muchmore outside 'Eleanor' in Margaret Avenue, late 1940s.

'Peacehaven' in Ronald Avenue being built in 1936.

plotlanders will tell you how it was perfectly safe to leave supplies on the plots as no one would ever touch anything. However, the owner of 'Homeleigh' in Third Avenue told me that around 1939 they had sufficient materials delivered to build a good-sized prefab building. It was the sort designed for troops, made from wood with asbestos sheets lining the inside and shiplap timber on the outside. Unfortunately someone stole a quantity of wood and they could then only manage to build a smaller dwelling.

Not all properties were designed by the owners. It was also possible to buy a kit for a bungalow from a catalogue. You could either pay for a local builder to erect it, or erect it yourself. This is what Marion Allwood's family (the Muchmores) did in 1935 when her father and uncle built 'Eleanor' in Margaret Avenue.

When it came to adding those little finishing touches the plotlanders were a resourceful bunch, as can be seen from Dave Anderson's memories of maintenance work on his grandparents' bungalow 'Iris Villa' in Beech Hall Gardens:

The bungalow was a timber-framed building built onto a solid cement base. It was clad with tongue and groove timber on the bottom half, which was painted black, and the top half was clad in asbestos sheeting painted white. I remember my father telling me that in the Second World War paint was in short supply, so as he was in the printing business he painted the bungalow with black printers' ink!

The 'bungalow' originated in India and had become very popular in the interwar years.[1] One feature much loved by plotlanders was the veranda. 'Veranda' was a Hindi word for the area surrounding the dwelling which helped to give some shelter from the sun and heat. I doubt that the temperatures in Essex quite matched the heat of India, but no plotland dwelling was complete without one. Even if a hut didn't start off with a veranda, it often ended up with one.

Plotlanders just couldn't stop tinkering and improving their properties. Indeed, it seems that even when you took plotlanders out of the plotlands and put them into a new Corporation house,

Laying the footings for 'Edelweiss' on Lower Avenue, with Merrylands Farmhouse in the distance (1930s/40s).

'Iris Villa' in Beech Hall Gardens, 1950s.

you couldn't take the plotlands out of the plotlanders. At its meeting on 8 March 1973 Basildon Development Corporation considered a report by the General Manager on the increasing number of alterations being carried out by purchasers of Corporation homes. People had begun to add porches (probably as a precursor to a veranda), fences around open front gardens and even made more substantial structural alterations. The Corporation agreed to restrict control of these changes 'to safeguard the landscape and street picture'. It even produced a leaflet to explain what residents could and could not do to their homes.[2]

Photos and descriptions of plotland developments on the east and south coasts show plenty of examples of old railway carriages, van bodies and trams being used as abodes. Looking at the Corporation's 1949 survey of the Dunton plotlands I could find no mention of any ex-modes of transport being used as dwellings. Either they were very well disguised, or they had become defunct by the late 1940s and been replaced by more permanent dwellings, or they had not been so common in this area. It was possibly a combination of all three.

Nonetheless, I have come across a few accounts of unconventional dwellings. For example, a news article from 1931 referred to a dwelling in Berry Drive which was described as 'the top of a van which rested on the ground so as to form a hut'.[3] Tom Wallace recalls living in a converted railway carriage in New Century Road in the 1940s, and a resident of 'The Roost' in Bridge Avenue described having a single-decker bus in the garden.[4]

Nina Humphrey's family used an old London tram as additional accommodation and a playroom on their plot. However, this wasn't mentioned in the survey of 'Spion Kop', so perhaps the surveyors chose to disregard anything that was additional to the main form of accommodation. Nina's brother Dennis explained that in the 1920s or 1930s two trams were brought down from London, either by road or freight train. One went to their neighbour in 'The Retreat'. Once they were put in place the cast-iron wheels were removed and taken back to London because they were worth a lot of money. At 'Spion Kop' the tram was attached to the bungalow and boarding was used to blend it with the rest of the building. In later years it was moved away from the building and left free-standing.

When it came to building the housing for Basildon New Town it appears that flat-roofed buildings suddenly became very popular in the 1960s. I can't help but worry that it might have been caused by some wandering architect taking a fancy to our plot, 'Halliford' in High Bank Drive. If so, I unreservedly offer my apologies. Perhaps I can try sharing some of the blame, because Gladys Fenn's family plot, 'Rose Villa' in Hill Top

Ready for an afternoon of DIY
on Hillcrest Avenue, late 1930s.

Ex-London tram attached
to the right-hand side of
'Spion Kop', *c.*1953.

Rise, was another flat-roofer that might have turned the odd architect's head.

Indeed, in a global recession the design of 'Rose Villa' might turn out to be inspirational once again. The hut itself started out life as a large packing crate, so if the shipping trade doesn't pick up perhaps we shall all be living in old shipping containers in the future. Just in case (pardon the pun), let's get advice from Gladys Fenn on how her grandfather adapted it to make a cosy dwelling:

> In the mid-1930s my Grandfather ordered an empty
> wooden crate to be delivered by truck to the site.
> The crate had previously been used to import a car
> from abroad. He set the crate on old railway sleepers
> that he would have obtained from the railway yard in
> Leytonstone where he kept his horses that pulled his coal
> cart. The crate was just a huge wooden box that opened
> sideways. He then added a small window to one side.

Amazingly, this structure was one of the last weekend properties to survive on the High Bank Estate and was still there until 1984, when it was most likely pushed over by vandals. However, the wooden floor lasted for another 18 months after that. Gladys explained that the timber for the railway sleepers had probably come from the Baltic to Lowestoft, where they would have been soaked in creosote, thus helping them to survive for another 50 years in the plotlands. Their story did not finish in Hill Top Rise, as they ended up being transported to one of the last inhabited properties at the top of the Avenues on the Dunton Hills Estate. Nothing ever went to waste in the plotlands!

Next we will look at the survey of plotland properties which took place in 1949/50, and begin to build our portrait of the area.

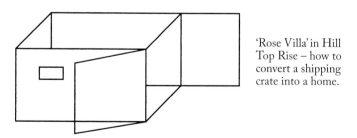

'Rose Villa' in Hill Top Rise – how to convert a shipping crate into a home.

Not much escaped the bulldozers – remains of plots on the Dunton Hills Estate in 2010.

Chapter 2

The 1949/50 Plotland Survey

Much of the detailed information about the plots and lanes described in this book has come from Basildon Development Corporation files. As one of its first acts the Corporation commissioned an 'Age and Condition Survey' of property in the area designated for the New Town.[1] During the autumn and winter of 1949 and the spring of 1950 a team of surveyors trudged around the area earmarked for development or inclusion in the Master Plan for Basildon. This was quite a task as in addition to made-up roads there were around 75 miles of grass tracks.[2] Their job was to describe the state of each lane and each plot of land.

The 1951 technical report which accompanied the Master Plan showed that there were 8,716 dwellings in the area, of which 2,045 were brick and tile and met the 1936 Housing Act Standards (HAS); 1,003 were light structures also meeting the HAS; 823 were brick and tile below the HAS; 1,115 were light structures below the HAS; 1,847 were chalets or shacks in good condition; 1,170 were judged to be bad in terms of structure and condition; and 713 were classed as very bad structures or were derelict.[3]

When I first discovered the original maps and surveyors' notes at Essex Records Office I wanted to run the length of the Readers' Room whooping and dancing. It was only a few weeks later that I reflected on the fact that the survey hadn't been written for my delight, nor for the benefit of history. Its purpose had been to inform the Corporation of the extent of the task it faced in building the new town. The majority of these meticulously recorded plots would ultimately fall before the bulldozer. Suddenly the survey felt more like a farmer's inventory of his turkeys in the run-up to Christmas.

So why did I get so excited about these documents? You are probably thinking it's because I clearly don't get out much, but there is more to it than that. These documents represent a snapshot of the plotlands at a key moment in their history, just before they began to disappear. The number of people residing in the area was at its peak and would never be as high again. On these sheets the surveyors recorded the names of the plots (where they were known); a description of the building; an estimate of the number of rooms; an estimate of the lifespan of the building; a judgement of its architectural quality and condition; and an overall comment about the state of the whole plot. On the accompanying maps the surveyors had marked the position of every plot, so with a little imagination it is possible to reconstruct an image of what each lane looked like.

It is worth emphasising that the survey is just a snapshot of the area at one moment in time. Just because some plots were described as derelict, it did not mean that they had permanently fallen out of use. My family's own plot, 'Halliford', was unnamed in the survey and described as being derelict and overgrown, with a timber and felt hut on it. However, it sprang into life again when my parents bought it in 1954. Members of my family alone bought five plots on the High Bank Estate in the 1950s, and I have met other people who purchased plots in the 1950s and early 1960s, which shows there was still a market for weekend properties in the post-war period.

There is one important piece of information missing from the surveys – they do not give the owner's name. However, we have gained further details from Electoral Registers and from talking to former residents. It soon became clear that it was very common for several members of the same family to own plots in one lane or neighbouring lanes.

Wellies and Clipboards

I couldn't help wondering what it must have been like for the surveyors undertaking this unique task. According to the sheets, the surveyors in these areas were named K. Munnich, H. Bonwick, Ray Stokes, R.L. Mantall, Oldfield, S.G. Turner and J.G. Lane. I imagined them all to be men with clipboards, dressed in heavy over-coats, trilby hats and trousers tucked into wellington boots. Of course, apart from Ray they could have been a team of women – but I doubt it. Nevertheless, if you prefer to picture a bevy of beauties in the best figure-hugging winter outfits that post-war Essex shops could offer, then be my guest.

When the first survey was conducted in lanes around Laindon in early autumn 1949 it may have seemed quite a pleasant task. Essex was experiencing something of an Indian summer that year, so wandering

around grassy lanes in the warm glow of the autumn sun probably didn't seem too bad. The blackberries would have been at their juicy best, purple Michaelmas Daisies would have nodded at the surveyors from the 'neat' or 'well-kept' plots, and wayward long stems of grass would have cast a curious eye at the passers-by from the runaway lawns of the 'unkept' front gardens. Did Ray Stokes first think to himself that this wasn't too bad an assignment? I wonder whether his mood had changed by 28 December as he negotiated round the puddles in Helmore Crescent. Trudging along Bridge Avenue on 20 December, possibly with hands too cold to grasp a pencil, did H. Bonwick wonder what on earth he had done to deserve this job? Were there any signs in the inhabited bungalows and shacks that Christmas was only a couple of days away? Were the residents' geese or turkeys looking a bit anxious?

I haven't met anyone who remembers these surveyors doing their rounds, and I wonder if it felt threatening to see someone with a clipboard standing outside your property. How would the owners have felt to know that their pride and joy was being described as being of 'architecturally poor' condition, and the plot as 'untidy'? Even 60 years on, my co-writer Peter's first comment when he saw the description of his family's plot in Hillcrest Avenue was, 'I was rather surprised to see the modest description of "Wendover" as being "kept" rather than "well-kept".' Clearly a modest description could still rankle after all those years.

Peter also made an interesting point about the accuracy of the survey. When surveyed on 20 December 1949 'Wendover' was described as being a wooden building in a fair condition, with a tile roof and an estimated two rooms. Peter said,

> to my knowledge in 1949 it had at least four rooms (bedroom, large hall/sleeping space, smaller store room, living room, kitchen and a huge loft space with a purpose-built counter-balanced wooden retractable ladder). Also it had a pebble-dash render on probably wood-framed walls with a solid brick foundation and a proper tiled roof. If fact I still have a piece of the brick from the foundations on my rockery.

Beech Hall Gardens in 1950s –
typical lane with scattered development.

We should perhaps bear in mind that not all details in the survey might be entirely accurate. I also wonder how much guidance the surveyors were given when describing the more subjective elements, such as the condition of the plot. Did they have a moderation meeting between the team members to decide the difference between 'kept' and 'well kept', 'tidy', and 'very tidy', 'fair', 'fair +', and 'fair -'?

I have only come across one example where two different surveyors surveyed the same property. This was 'Varfor' in Fourth Avenue (Dunton Hills Estate) which was surveyed on 3 February 1950 and 5 April 1950. It received the following descriptions, which show that opinions differed:

No. of rooms	Building material	Roof	Condition of building in 1949	Condition of plot in 1949	Date of survey
3	Concrete block asbestos	Tile	Fair +	Fairly well kept	3/2/50
3	Brick rendered	Tile	Good	Well cared for	5/4/50

I have met Clive Layton, whose grandparents were living in 'Varfor' at the time, and his memories are given in the next chapter.

What did the Surveyors find?

I studied the surveys for over 620 plots, focussing my attention on four areas: the Dunton Hills Estate (which is now part of the Langdon Nature Reserve, and where Peter's family plots were located); the western corner of Laindon to the north of the railway line (which I remember going under the bulldozer in the 1970s); the Berry Park Estate; and the High Bank Estate (where my family's plot 'Halliford' was located).

With very few exceptions the buildings were judged to be of architecturally poor quality, and the majority were judged to have less than 20 years' worth of life left. Most lanes were unmade, and only a few were lit by gas lamps.

Looking at the details of the survey on a lane-by-lane basis, it became clear that some parts of the plotland estates were primarily used by weekenders with their one-roomed wooden huts, but other sections had a high percentage of permanent residents with more substantial dwellings. In later chapters, we will look at the character of particular lanes. However, overall, 43 per cent of the properties I studied were judged to have one room, 24 per cent two rooms and 33 per cent three or more rooms.

The descriptions of the building material showed that 67 per cent of properties were made of timber or wood and were not rendered, and six per cent were brick. Twenty-seven per cent were rendered with stucco or pebbledash, but the surveyors had often noted that the basic structure was wood. Just over half

the properties had tiled roofs (normally asbestos tiles); 28 per cent had felt roofs; seven per cent corrugated iron; eight per cent slates; and four per cent used materials such as asbestos sheets.

The majority of plots were 'kept' (in some fashion). Only a small number seemed to be completely 'derelict'. However, many lanes also contained wasteland or empty plots which possibly had never been occupied.

'Varfor' in Fourth Avenue, mid-1940s. Note the steep slope of the hill.

What was the Outcome of the Survey?

A preliminary report on the Age and Condition Survey was prepared by the Chief Architect's Department to look at the financial and legal aspects arising from the clearance of 'shacks' in the designated area. It was given the snappy title 'Shack Clearance: a preliminary view of the problem' and was sent to the Corporation's meeting on 7 July 1950. The report stated that any property judged to have a life of less than 20 years had been classified as a shack, and approximately 5,000 properties met this description. There were plenty of other dwellings in the area which were of a more substantial nature, and therefore not included in this category.

The main question posed by the report was what the Corporation should do about all these 'shacks'. While not offering any concrete proposals (although smothering most things with concrete seemed to be the ultimate answer) the report highlighted a number of points for consideration.

The designated area for the New Town included land that was earmarked for development (whether it be residential, commercial, or industrial); land for recreational use; and land that would probably be returned for agricultural use. The latter tended to be outside what the Corporation called the 'urban fence'. The existing properties were scattered inside and outside this urban fence.

The report noted that different approaches may be needed depending on the location of the plots, and divided up the problem into three parts:

> Category I consists of approximately 1,300 shacks outside the urban fence of the draft Master Plan, in scattered development without roads or drains and on land difficult to develop.
>
> Category II consists of some 2,500 shacks inside the urban fence of the draft Master Plan in areas where complete redevelopment will be necessary. Development is scattered; in most cases there are neither roads nor drains and few services; moreover the existing 'grass' street pattern is quite unsuitable for retention.

'Gladioli' – a one-roomed weekend hut near Dry Street, owned by Maud Barry.

Category III includes about 1,200 shacks inside the urban fence of the draft Master Plan in areas where the street pattern will probably be retained owing to its existing capital value.[4]

The shacks in the Dunton Hills area would have fallen into Category I. Those in lanes to the north of the railway (such as Alexandra Road, Helmore Crescent and Victory Avenue) would most likely have come into Category II. Only dwellings in roads close to Laindon High Road may have fallen into Category III.

Accommodating people who were dispossessed of their land was a major issue for the Corporation, especially in the early days before it had built any houses of its own. The New Towns and the Town and Country Planning Acts both contained legislation on how to treat people who had lost their freehold rights. The former Act stated that residents must be given 'the opportunity to be re-accommodated on reasonable terms and an absolute right to have alternative residential accommodation before displacement'. The latter act included an amendment to state that the accommodation must be 'suitable to their reasonable requirements'.[5] In other words a spinster living in a mansion could not claim that she should be provided with a similar-sized property.

The report posed the question of whether clearing plots in Category I should be the Corporation's responsibility, given that the land was not earmarked for development. Clearance of the area would be costly since it would involve compensation for the loss of the owners' property, rehousing dispossessed people and demolishing the buildings. On the other hand, simply doing nothing would not address the Corporation's original intention to bring some kind of order to the unplanned chaos of scattered plotland development. If the Corporation didn't tackle this, then who would?

Of course, the Corporation could legitimately decide to delay tackling this issue for a couple of decades as it had enough on its hands dealing with the 3,700 shacks (and other properties not classed as shacks) within the urban fence. However, the report noted that if no control was exercised in these areas, there would be 'a natural tendency for such areas to consolidate and increase in value by way of extensions to the buildings themselves'.[6]

It became apparent that the Corporation decided not to try biting off more than it could chew, and to leave clearance of many of the Category I plots until it had completed the development elsewhere. Indeed it did not turn its attention back to Laindon and Dunton until the late 1960s, when it published its first draft of the South West Area Plan. As we will see in our final chapter, it was as late as the 1980s when the Corporation finally returned to the issue of what to do with the handful of shack dwellers still left on the Dunton Hills Estate.

What's in a Name?

I was delighted that the surveyors included the name of the property where they were able to find one. Sometimes the spelling was unclear and in some cases I think the surveyors misread the name, as I have found slight discrepancies with the name given in 1950 Electoral Register and from the details that ex-plotlanders can recall. Not all plots retained the same name as they had done in 1949. New owners often changed the name, or named the unnamed plots. For example 'Jocelyn' in High View Avenue became 'Bonanza' in 1962.

Worthing Road in the 1940s – a typical unmade lane.

The Andersons at 'Bonanza' in 1967. Perhaps they need a new deckchair to go with the new name?

There is something special about discovering the names. They help to evoke the character of the owners and say something about their aspirations. I have been fortunate that ex-plotlanders have helped me to decode some of them, as at first sight they seemed very odd.

A number of patterns emerge when you look at all the names, and trying to guess their origin is half the fun. By far the most popular were names involving 'Rose' in some way – leaving us with several Rose Cottages, Rosedenes and Rosemounts; a whole host of Rosemaries/Rosemarys; and appearances from Rose View, Rosecroft, Rosebud, Roseville, Irene Rose, Rose Villa, The Rose, Roselyn, Roselandia, Rosedale and Rose Garden.

These few examples also illustrate another popular practice whereby owners added 'Dene', 'View', 'Ville' and 'Villa' to the end of names to spice them up a bit.

Unsurprisingly, names evoking tranquillity, the notion of a rural idyll and nature were also popular. Examples include 'Haven of Rest' (owned by the Mays in Berry Drive), 'Shangri-la' (owned by the Lambdens of Arcadian Gardens), and 'The Elms' (Ronald Avenue).

Many names simply reflect the location of the plot, such as 'Clear View', 'Hill Top' and 'Hill Crest' on Hillcrest Avenue, whose names show that they were at the top of the hill with uninterrupted views across the Essex countryside as far as Kent and London. I can only imagine that 'Muddy Waters' in Crest Avenue was so named after the state of the road outside.

Many people named their plot after themselves, such as these examples from Beech Hall Gardens: 'Ray Villa' owned by Mr and Mrs Ray, 'Essex Villa' owned by Mr and Mrs Essex, and 'Iris Villa' named after Iris Anderson, the owner's daughter.

Some names had to be decoded for me by ex-plotlanders, who explained that the name was a combination of the husband's surname and the wife's maiden name. Hence we have 'Varfor' in Fourth Avenue (Vardy and Forman); 'Carncastle' in Helmore Crescent (Carnell and Hardcastle); and 'Clemrich' in King Edward Road (Clements and Richards). There are also those which when read backwards give the name of the owner – such as these two from Helmore Crescent: 'Se Kaon' (Noakes) and 'Eltrym' (Myrtle).

There are those named after the road in which the owners normally lived – such as our own 'Halliford' in High Bank Drive, named after Halliford Street in Islington, or 'Whitethorn' in Highland Gardens, named after Whitethorn Road in Bow.

Peter explains that 'Wendover' and 'Coombe Cottage' were named after his family's favourite holiday locations. I suspect this may also be the origin for plots such as 'St Ives' in Second Avenue and 'Torbay' in Helmore Crescent.

Sometimes names had a deeper meaning. The late Allan Young's family owned 'Lansbury' in Fourth Avenue and according to Allan his father's 'early socialist principles embraced the outdoor life, self reliance and effort'. The plot was named in honour of George Lansbury, one of his father's 'admired early socialists'.[7]

Among my favourites were the atmospheric names like 'The Lair' (Helmore Crescent) and the light-hearted ones like 'Hammers Rest' (Hillcrest Avenue), 'N'Gonna' (Helmore Crescent), 'Erz-n-myne' (owned by the Renwick Family in Bridge Avenue) and the bizarre 'High Elm Hickaloo' (Berry Drive). I also liked the sound of snug little 'Airtight Cottage' in Lower Avenue which was named in a wartime survey.

A Tale of Two Surveys

In the next chapter we will start to look at the various plotland estates in more detail, but I wanted to make one final comment about the 1949 survey and compare it with another survey which we will also be considering in this book. Only seven years earlier Charles Leatherland (later to become Lord Leatherland) had conducted a wartime survey of local properties for the Dunton Parish Invasion Committee. The aim of that survey was to identify resources which could be used in the defence of plotland homes against their destruction by Hitler's Master Race. Ironically, the aim of the 1949 survey was to identify plotland homes for destruction by Basildon's Master Plan …

A view over the Dunton Hills Estate as Walter Firman works on 'Vera-Joan' in Hillcrest Avenue, late 1940s.

Chapter 3

The Dunton Hills Estate

We'll start our tour of plotland estates with a look at the Dunton Hills Estate. This is the only part of the plotlands which has been retained in Basildon, and will be familiar to anyone who has visited the Langdon Nature Reserve on Third Avenue, just off Lower Dunton Road. The area was saved from development by the efforts of local objectors, and by its topography and geology. In the 1970 version of the South West Area Plan, the planners noted that the west-facing London clay slope 'exhibits unmistakable signs of past land slipping' and concluded that it would be 'prudent to leave it completely undeveloped'.[1]

The 1949 survey showed that there were over 154 properties on this estate (excluding Lower Dunton Road); 36 per cent of these were estimated to be one-roomed, 36 per cent two-roomed and 29 per cent with three or more rooms. It also showed that 60 per cent were of wood/timber construction, 29 per cent rendered timber, eight per cent brick and three per cent other (e.g., caravans).[2]

The area today has been transformed since the mid-1920s when the former farmland was divided up and sold at auction. Photos from the late 1930s and 1940s still show the Dunton Hills Estate as a grassy open landscape, but in the last half-century nature has gradually reclaimed the land. Michael Anthony recalls that there were very few trees on the estate in the 1940s and 1950s, apart from planted fruit trees. 'There was nothing to spoil our view of the gorgeous sunsets when the sun sunk behind the heavily polluted air of London.'

Thanks to the work of the staff and volunteers of Essex Wildlife Trust it is still possible to walk along the lanes. The land was purchased by the Trust in the late 1980s with the help of a memorial bequest from Herbert Langdon Dowsett, who was a local surveyor and keen conservationist. The first warden, Nigel Wood, temporarily moved into 'Hawthorn' on Hillcrest Avenue after the Burke family moved out.

As a member of Basildon Natural History Society, Colin Humphrey recalls that several members of the Corporation's Planning Department were very helpful in pushing for the establishment of the reserve and for preserving 'The Haven' on Third Avenue as a plotland museum. Indeed, for many years the Natural History Society had been holding regular meetings with Corporation staff to discuss the establishment and management of other reserves, such as Marks Hill.

In the 1980s Colin recalls meetings being held in 'Hawthorn' to discuss the management of the new Langdon Reserve. 'We sat in the dim kitchen which was lit by a 12 volt powered fluorescent tube. The wind was howling round the bungalow and blowing under the gaps in the door, making the lino flap up and down. It was very atmospheric.'

Much has been written about the Dunton Hills Estate so we are only focusing on a few plots to give the spirit of time passed. Although the sites of the former plots are mostly overgrown with dense hawthorn scrub and trees, the outlines of gardens can still be made out in some places. Rubble and the remnants of everyday items can sometimes be found lurking in the heart of bushes.

Fourth Avenue

According to the 1949 survey there were at least 17 properties in this lane, which runs up the hill. Twelve were described as timber/wood, of which five were rendered. The rest were brick/concrete. Those properties on the right-hand side backed onto fields.

'Anthelen'

Michael Anthony's grandfather Joseph Anthony bought this plot at the top of Fourth Avenue in the 1930s as a weekend retreat. Its name was a pun based on his surname and the fact that his wife's first name was Ellen but everyone called her 'Aunt Nell'. During the war the family's home in Stepney was destroyed, so they had to move to 'Anthelen' permanently. Unfortunately Joseph died in

Anthony Family outside the new bungalow at 'Anthelen', *c*. 1940.

1941 but Ellen remained living there until she died in 1962. Their daughter, Joan, married a stonemason called Mr Arnold and lived in a bungalow at the bottom of Fourth Avenue called 'Carrara' until the 1960s.

Michael explains that there were two bungalows on the site of 'Anthelen':

> There was the old bungalow to the rear that was a small converted garage structure intended originally for weekend use. The 'new' bungalow was at the front of the plot and it wasn't completely finished until after the war. It was on a very steep slope, so the foundations had to be dug into the hillside on one side.

In the 1949 survey 'Anthelen' was described as being a 'three roomed timber rendered building in a fair condition with a tile roof'. It had a 'fairly well kept garden'. The neighbouring plot was a narrow strip of neglected scrubland.

The bungalow gradually deteriorated and correspondence with insurance companies in the 1960s relate to claims for damage caused by severe dampness and fire. Michael's parents eventually sold the plot in 1985 to the Corporation. A neighbour recalls that 'Anthelen' was still standing until it fell down in the mid-1970s and at one time there were two people squatting in it for about six months. When he discovered the plotlands in 1984 Mark McManus described coming across this plot:

> Deep within the trees of Fourth Avenue once stood a house called 'Anthelen'. Apparently the house had previously been demolished, but a large wooden shack in the back garden remained standing. This shack, painted blue and divided into two equally sized rooms and a porch, possessed an eerie, ethereal quality as it stood quietly dappled in sunlight. This old building succumbed to a fire in 1985.

'Varfor'

'Varfor' stood a few plots down from 'Anthelen'. Clive Layton recalls his stays as a young boy with his grandparents who owned the plot:

> My father had helped to draw plans for the original hut when my grandparents bought the plot before the War. The original hut was at the end of the garden just in front of the outside toilet. When they added the new bungalow it was built on a steep slope, as one side of the plot was much lower than the other. The plot also sloped quickly to the rear, and there were several sets of steps in

the garden to take you down to the toilet. On the bungalow there were stone steps leading from the back door which went down to a coal cellar where we also kept food as it was very cool. The living room was above it.

There were strange empty squares in the wall of the building, and odd pipes which went nowhere. Later I realised that my granddad had included them because he had assumed electricity and gas would arrive, but it never did. Likewise in the garden there was a mysterious wooden square, surrounded by brown tiles – which was ready for a toilet with the huge space below, presumably for a septic tank. The ruins are still visible today.

Granddad still worked in Barking as a foreman at Masters' Match Factory, and he travelled by train every day, walking from the station, across Great Berry to the Avenues. After he retired in the late 1940s he had more time so he also cultivated his younger son's plot (on Fourth Avenue opposite the short cut) and so, with their vegetables and fruit trees and bushes (for jam-making) they never needed to buy basics except meat, but even then they had rabbits, chickens and geese.

William Vardy outside 'Varfor' in 1942.

Ruins of 'Varfor' still visible in 2010.

Clive Layton outside 'Varfor' in Fourth Avenue in the mid-1940s.

'Violet Lodge' being built in 1938 – view of the rear.

Walking up Fourth Avenue I would look for the very tall pole on which my granddad would fly the Red Ensign which had been given to him by the ship's captain when he was invalided out as an engineer with severe scalding. He then joined the army and survived Gallipoli. The flag pole was still there long after he died.

As an early teenager I suddenly realised, one clear sunny summer's day, that the ships I could see in the distance were in fact at Tilbury Docks. The 'Strath' and Orient Line ships were distinctive – the latter by colour and number of funnels. I had toured over these ships on Sundays as my father, a tally clerk, was able to get passes.

We had a few neighbours in the lane. Reg and 'Owl' Folkhard were, I believe, my dad's cousins and they lived at 'Violet Lodge'. I was in my mid-teens before I realised that 'Owl' was an abbreviation in 'East Lunnon tawk' for Alice!

The side of the empty plot next to them was a path to the 'rabbit field' in which hay or clover was grown and cut twice a year. There was a diagonal path which led to the end of Hillcrest Avenue, which was known locally as 'The Dip' or 'The Dipping'. The people who lived along there kept to themselves – mysterious.

My grandparents had both died by 1957 and were buried in Little Burstead Church. We didn't go to the plot

'Beauty' from 'Landview' roaming along the top of Second Avenue – 'Clearview' seen in distance.

much after that, but I returned in 2009 and was amazed to find remnants among the undergrowth.

Clive also recalled the following incident, which was common in the plotlands:

> There was a plot at the corner of Central Avenue and Second Avenue where you could buy newspapers on Sundays. I used to go to fetch them. One day there was a fierce dog loose in Central Avenue and I couldn't pass it so I had to go up Second Avenue, along Hillcrest and back down Fourth to get home. There were always dogs wandering about.

When walking past plots it was common to hear the sound of ferocious barking from within or, even more worryingly, to see a large mutt racing down the path towards a flimsy-looking fence. In some areas dogs would have the free run of the lane, making that section a virtual no-go area for the timid. There were certain lanes we would never dare walk down because we knew dogs would be roaming around ready to challenge, and even bite, unsuspecting passers-by. In the 1970s I remember a couple of dogs regularly coming round to our plot 'to play' or to scavenge food. We didn't know who owned them, but thankfully they seemed harmless enough. In the latter days of the plotlands, many elderly people were living alone and a dog was essential for companionship and security.

'The Plot'

Ken Royden's grandmother came from Bow and she purchased several plots just after the war. They remained in his family until the Corporation compulsorily purchased the land after the hut burnt down in the mid-1980s:

If you walk up Fourth Avenue to Central Avenue, on the right the front area of the plot is still there pretty much clear. We also had the land at the back to the right so we had an L-shaped plot. This is all overgrown now. Our wooden building was built by my father sometime in the late 1940s who a few years later built a small extension on the back – which was never told to the council to avoid the rates. At the back of our plot there are the remains of an old wooden boat which I put there in the late 1970s when the area was clear. There is also an Anderson shelter at the very back which was never dug in but used as a shed.

My uncle had the plot on the opposite side of the avenue. He had a wooden structure that he covered in ferro cement. I still remember the building standing but was unused by then. This was never officially demolished. The forest reclaimed it naturally. There are still some remains if you look carefully in the foliage. My aunt had the plot alongside ours but it was demolished officially before my memory.

I remember at the bottom of each avenue there was a gas light on a telephone post. At dusk a man used to come along and light each lamp. The council changed these over to electric light in the very early 1970s.

Fourth Avenue was quite popular and there were many bungalows on the avenue but most people did not keep them going for very long and they disappeared rather more quickly than other avenues. I knew the people who lived in 'Hawthorn' on Hillcrest Avenue very well. They used to take in any abandoned unwanted animals. They had dogs, cats including a Siamese, sheep, goats etc. When they sold, the council moved them to

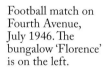

Football match on Fourth Avenue, July 1946. The bungalow 'Florence' is on the left.

Basildon. They did visit us on our plot some time later but they said although their house was new, modern and clean, they hated it.

There was a man named Dennis who lived halfway up the hill on the right with his wife, who had battery hen sheds at the rear. I remember going in the sheds with my family to buy eggs. When he closed this down he was a petrol attendant in Bulphan village. He sold up in the late 1960s and rented the house at the bottom of Fourth Avenue.

Down 'the dip' a lady known as Granny Smith had a lovely bungalow – large for the area. I remember talking to her with my family in the late 1960s. She had a bull nose Morris, which the foliage was taking over. She said I could have it if I wanted it but we never had a vehicle to pull it up the dip, which was very steep. When my father bought a Landrover in 1973 we went back down there. Granny Smith had since died by then and the bungalow demolished – the car had also been taken. Just my luck!

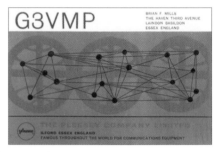

Promotional card for Brian Mills' electronics business at 'The Haven'.

Brian Mills outside 'The Haven' – now the Plotland Museum.

Third Avenue

In 1949 there were 29 properties in the lane; 28 were described as being constructed from timber/wood, of which 10 were rendered. There was one brick bungalow.

'The Haven'

Only 'The Haven', the former home of the Mills Family and now the Plotland Museum on Third Avenue, remains on the entire estate. Mena and Frederick Mills bought the property in 1934.[3] Their family continued to live there until 1983. In the 1970s one of their sons, Brian, even ran a small electronics business from home. His impressive advertising postcard makes it look like 'The Haven' was located in 'Silicon Valley' rather than 'Gumboot Hill'!

First, Second and Stack Avenues

Like other avenues on the estate, these were all grassy unmade roads. The 1949 survey revealed how many properties they contained: Second Avenue – 29; First Avenue – 16; Stack Avenue – seven larger properties, all of which had four or more rooms. I believe Stack Avenue was established before the other avenues came into existence, hence the larger size of the dwellings.

Three of the plots in Stack Avenue ('Homestead', 'Shanklin' and 'Bracknell') belonged to members of the Jenkins family, who were all keen on keeping chickens. The land is now part of the Langdon Lake and Meadow Reserve and its warden (Mick Coulson) recently found the remains of old chicken-feeding equipment in the undergrowth.

Hillcrest Avenue

This was a long avenue running horizontally across the top of the estate from the junction of First Avenue and Margaret Avenue to the north, beyond Fourth Avenue to the south and falling away steeply into 'The Dip', where it ended at a small stream that runs along a field boundary in a deep ditch. The stream eventually flows into the Mar Dyke that crosses Bulphan Fen on its way to the Thames at Purfleet.

In 1949 there were 56 properties in the lane: 26 were estimated to have one room; 22 two rooms; and eight three or more rooms. Forty-five were described as being timber/wood huts or bungalows; seven were rendered timber; two brick; one asbestos sheets; and one concrete slabs. Several properties lasted until 1985, when they were bought in accordance with the final Compulsory Purchase Order for the area.

In the next chapter Peter Jackson will give us his memories of his family's and friends' plots on Hillcrest Avenue.

'Vera-Joan' on
Hillcrest Avenue.

Chapter 4

A Tale of Three Plots
Peter's Story

In the 1930s my paternal grandparents, Sidney and Rebecca Jackson, bought 'Wendover' on Hillcrest Avenue on the Dunton Hills Estate as a weekend retreat. My father, Wallace, actually met my mother, Joan Firman, at Dunton as her family owned 'Vera-Joan' next door.

By the 1950s my parents and I lived in Upton Park in a largish Victorian terraced house. We occupied the downstairs rooms while my grandparents were upstairs with their lodger and family friend, Harry Salmon, who had the large room at the front of the house. Harry owned 'Coombe Cottage' next to 'Wendover'. Today, these properties are part of the Langdon Wildlife Reserve, overgrown with trees and slashed through by a new path. Here are some memories of their heyday.

'Vera-Joan'

My grandfather, Walter Firman, worked in a public house in Leicester Square, London, where it was the nature of his job to be constantly in touch with the local gossip and news. Somehow he became infected with the enthusiasm he saw around him for the opportunities to buy land outside London where you could spend time in the country, away from the thick air and noise. He became so enthusiastic that my grandmother, Lucy, was always having to put a damper on some of his wilder schemes, always worried that he would buy another plot behind her back.

In 1933 he did succeed in buying the land on Hillcrest Avenue, which he named after his two daughters. It cost him £20 for two plots of land and he bought it on easy payment terms – £2 down and 10s. per month with five per cent interest. It would have taken him over three years to pay for it, but he was immensely proud of the achievement.

Initially, his treasured purchase consisted of a large plot of overgrown grassland overlooking a strangely open view across the Avenues with their sporadic development. The family erected a bell tent and a pattern of weekends and holidays began that was to last for a good 30 more years.

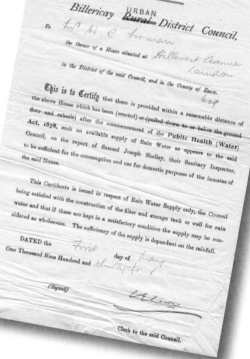

Clockwise from top left:

Walter Firman and an early version of 'Vera-Joan'.

Guests at 'Vera-Joan', mid-1930s.

Certificate of Water Supply, 'Vera-Joan', 1934.

Sub-lieutenant Kenneth Neale on leave at 'Vera-Joan'.

The next phase involved a little more permanence in the shape of first one shed, then two, and finally the construction of a two-room bungalow with kitchen extension. The builder that Walter engaged for the project made serious mistakes with the foundations which mattered a great deal in the heavy clay soil of the area. It was always said in the family that Walter was very angry with the builder and made strenuous efforts to get things put right. I do not know whether the building was underpinned or whether more drastic remedial work was carried out, but in the 1960s I was always struck by the strange angle of the long chimney stack as it jutted out from the wall of the living room.

Walter always took an active role with other residents in campaigning for facilities for the Dunton Hills Estate, attending meetings and writing letters. Gas and water mains were eventually laid to the property and things were looking brighter.

Possessing a 'place in the country' meant that many friends and relatives stayed for weekends and short holidays, experiencing its special atmosphere. In common with the owners of hundreds of other plotland properties, the Firmans had a large extended family in London who visited 'Vera-Joan' over the years, adding to the depth of memories that remain around this patch of ground. For many ex-plotlanders the war years added extra dimensions of drama and in this respect 'Vera-Joan' was no exception. Here are a few of the stories …

Lucy's nephew, Kenneth Neale, stayed at the bungalow in the 1940s, on leave from the navy. As a preparation for officer training, Kenneth had been drafted as an able seaman for six months on board the destroyer HMS *Firedrake*, on convoy escort duty. A few months after he had been transferred to a shore establishment, the ship was torpedoed in the North Atlantic by U211, with the loss of virtually the whole crew. Later, attached to the battleship HMS *Anson*, he witnessed the surrender of the Japanese forces at Hong Kong and saw the devastation in Yokohama and Tokyo. After the war, Kenneth had a distinguished career in the civil service, being awarded the OBE in 1959 and finally becoming Assistant Under Secretary of State in the Home Office, 1976-82.

Wallace Jackson, youngest son of the family next door in 'Wendover', returned from four years' service with the RAF in North Africa and Italy. He, too, had had his share of luck. In his case it was at an improvised landing ground in the Western Desert when the Wellington bomber on which he had been working blew up while being loaded with bombs. A few moments previously, he had just finished servicing one of the engines and walked a short distance away to the NAAFI hut for a tea break. The remaining ground crew were all killed. Wallace married Joan Firman in 1947.

Joan's friend May married Patrick, an air-gunner in the Fleet Air Arm, and the two of them spent time at 'Vera-Joan'. Pat told me of a time on operations, while he was sitting in the open rear gun position of a Swordfish biplane torpedo bomber, when he saw the tailplane being blown away by a direct hit from anti-aircraft fire.

*   *   *

Walter was always interested in gardening, and like many plotlanders he began to plant his property with fruit trees of all kinds, the more varied the better. By the time he admitted to himself that there was really no more room, there must have been at least 15 plum, damson, apple and pear trees.

When I came on the scene in the 1950s, these trees were mature and freely fruiting. The earliest apple was Beauty of Bath, a variety that to me was unique to Dunton

Walter Firman (left) in his garden with friend, Mr Woolley, 'Vera-Joan', late 1930s

and had a distinctive fresh flavour and appearance. A problem shared by most plotlanders with fruit trees was what to do with all the fruit, especially if, as in Walter's case, the planting had got a little out of hand. Bags of apples, pears and plums would be carried back along the paths to Laindon Station and then back to London. From the beginning of autumn, the bungalow always smelled of apples in store. A chore on arriving would be to sort through the fruit, discarding those that had turned the familiar brown with small white spots of rot appearing. A familiar dessert that I always associate with 'Vera-Joan' was stewed apple with blackberries, which we would easily gather from the many bramble bushes all around.

Walter died suddenly in 1951 from a heart attack. One of the results of this tragedy was that the large plot of ground in Dunton now presented a formidable amount of work. Lucy, with her daughters, their families and relatives, made valiant efforts to cut the grass and keep things in good order and repair, but this became increasingly difficult. Demands of work in the 1950s meant that little time could be given to essential maintenance and money was always in short supply.

We spent many weekends and extended breaks in the summer at 'Vera-Joan' in the 1950s. I remember lying on a camp bed in the small bedroom of 'Vera-Joan', having woken up early on a Saturday morning among all the freedom of a Dunton weekend, listening to the distant echoing sound of a steam train on the Southend to Fenchurch Street line. Above me on the wall was a print of 'Rebecca at the Well' in an ornate gold-painted oval frame. In front of the

camp bed, underneath a window that looked out over the view from the hill through a small veranda, was a heavy dressing table with a hinged mirror. The larger drawers were always very awkward to open, probably suffering from damp, and were mainly used to store apples or pears. Smaller upper drawers contained evidence of past times when the bungalow was used by the Firman family with their teenage daughters. I particularly remember a glass perfume spray, long discarded, but still containing traces of fragrance. Next to the chest of drawers was the front door to the right, never opened in all the time I stayed in the bungalow.

The living room contained armchairs, a dining table, a smaller table on which stood a battery radio in a semi-circular tin case, and a fireplace in the centre of the north wall. Lighting was by gas, with fragile gas mantles that created a delicate light at night, contributing to the special atmosphere of the bungalow.

There was a portable wind-up gramophone and some 78rpm records, such as 'A Little Bit of Cucumber' and 'My Old Iron Cross' by Harry Champion, the celebrated cockney music hall performer. Although at the time I was totally unaware of it, this relic of the First World War certainly held poignant memories for my grandmother, whose first husband was killed in Mesopotamia shortly before the 1918 armistice and was buried in a military cemetery near Baghdad. They had married in 1915 and had only a few months together before he was posted abroad, never returning to England.

Outside, tucked away to the right of the garden, a small hut screened by a trellis held the chemical toilet. Up some concrete steps was a small lawn in front of the start of the fruit trees that was a convenient place for sitting out in the summer. On the left of this lawn was a shed that leaned increasingly to the right as the 1960s progressed. Inside was kept the supply of coal and some deckchairs.

Lucy Firman at the kitchen window, 'Vera-Joan', early 1960s.

Next to the shed was the earth mound of the Anderson shelter, covered in May and June with the rampant white flowers of snow-in-summer. I used to enjoy climbing on this small hill, but could never really get inside the shelter since it always seemed to be flooded with water. I wondered what conditions must have been like when it was in use in the war. Today the concrete base can still be seen close to the west side of the new path that crosses the property.

Beyond the small lawn was a central path that led between numerous fruit trees to a larger area of lawn at the back of the property, with even more fruit trees. A back gate gave access to the rough land between 'Vera-Joan' towards Denehurst Gardens and Sunnyside Gardens. On either side of the avenue of fruit trees had been vegetable plots and soft fruit bushes, but after the death of my grandfather, these had been virtually impossible to maintain. The ubiquitous patch of pungent horse-radish, found in several plotland gardens, and a few unsuccessful gooseberry bushes were all that remained as the '50s merged into the '60s.

The front garden that extended up both sides of the bungalow was set to lawn bordered by several rose bushes of the older fragrant varieties. The trellis around the front gate had a climbing rose. On a summer's evening, it was very pleasant to enjoy all this perfume while looking out over the view from the hill. As it got darker, you could sometimes see lines of moving red and white dots from cars on the A127 Arterial, or a long moving line of illuminated tiny train windows on the railway.

When my Aunt Vera and her family moved to Southend, my grandmother decided that she could no longer rent the house in Pedro Street, Clapton, and that it would be best if she moved permanently to Dunton and 'Vera-Joan'. Also at that time, Wallace and Joan Jackson, with me, their son, moved from Upton Park to Shelley Avenue, Langdon Hills, a 20-minute walk from Hillcrest Avenue. This had the consequence that Sidney and Rebecca Jackson, my paternal grandparents, also decided to take up permanent residence in Dunton in 'Wendover', as did their lodger, Harry Salmon, who moved into 'Coombe Cottage'.

As the 1960s progressed, my grandmother's health and mobility made it increasingly difficult to manage on her own in the tiny bungalow. Finally, bowing to the inevitable, she moved to council accommodation in Shelley Avenue, Langdon Hills, and 'Vera-Joan' was consigned to the Basildon Master Plan.

'Wendover'

Before the 1930s my grandmother, Rebecca Jackson, had supplemented the family's income by playing piano in cinemas and it was probably this extra cash that had enabled them to buy land on the eastern side of Hillcrest Avenue, commanding a fine view from its elevated position at the top of the hill. The choice of this plot was undoubtedly influenced by several family holidays in the Chilterns in the vicinity of Wendover and the famous Coombe Hill, with its fine wooded countryside and stunning views from the Boer War Monument. It was no accident, then, that they chose to name their land 'Wendover'.

Like all the Dunton plots, 'Wendover' started as a large patch of overgrown pasture. The first building was a shed. Later, the family were able to arrange for the building of a fairly grand bungalow that had a kitchen, one large bedroom, a large entrance hall that could

Rebecca Jackson at the front gate of 'Wendover', late 1940s.

Rear view of 'Wendover'.

double as another bedroom, a smaller store room, a living room, kitchen and large conservatory across the back. Under the roof was a large loft space with two small windows and an up-and-over ladder with counterweights that had been made by my grandfather to his own design. Water was collected from the roof and stored in a large agricultural water tank, while waste water from the one sink in the kitchen was disposed of in the usual soak-away arrangement. A channel led from the drainpipe down the sloping garden, gradually allowing the 'grey water' to soak into the ground, and scenting the air in the immediate vicinity with a weird stale soapy aroma.

The conservatory, or 'veranda' as it was known, was the usual method of entry into the bungalow, through stable doors and then the kitchen door. To the right of the door on entry there was always a table with pot plants. A large settee occupied the far wall to the right. French doors, usually closed and locked, gave additional access to the garden and were opposite another set of French doors that led into the living room. Unfortunately, by the 1960s, the glazing of the veranda's roof had become a little unreliable and when it rained for an appreciable length of time, an assortment of cooking pots, basins and buckets appeared to catch the drips, usually with an interesting free-form percussive effect.

The kitchen was quite well appointed for a plotland property. To the left of the back door was the sink with cold tap and small Ascot gas water heater. This also doubled as personal washing facilities. My grandmother always bought the more expensive bathroom version of 'Lifebuoy' and its fragrance constantly hung in the air, except when cooking was taking place, especially the traditional Sunday roast or, my grandparents' favourite, 'bloaters'. My cousins and I often piled into the kitchen on hot summers' days demanding some of the orange squash that was kept by the sink – mixed with the Dunton tap water that always seemed ice-cold and delicious.

The living room was arranged around the fireplace that provided the main heating for 'Wendover'. Opposite, up against a bay window, was a large dining table with extending leaves, large carved ornate legs and four matching dining chairs. In a corner was a large wind-up gramophone cabinet on which stood the wireless with its accumulator and large high-tension battery.

With the gas lighting and pictures on the walls, the whole effect was a cosy timelessness dating from the 1930s or even earlier. Next to the French doors and within poking distance of the fire was the armchair reserved for my grandfather. After dinner at midday, he was always to be found in his armchair, enjoying his afternoon sleep. Opposite, in her armchair, my grandmother would be knitting, filling in a football pool coupon or reading. Every day they read the *Daily Sketch* but she was also fond of Dickens and Thackeray, encouraging me to pick up *Sketches by Boz*.

After the electricity generator had been installed, a 12-volt lighting system replaced the gas mantle and even a small black and white TV made its appearance, slowly coming to life with power from the batteries when turned on, and its picture often rolling unpredictably.

The first generator purchased was an ex-army machine that drank petrol at such a startling rate that it was eventually banished to the shed and the family reverted to gas lighting. It was far too powerful and my father used to say that it was capable of lighting a whole street. Several years later, a smaller generator

made its appearance in a purpose-built lean-to on the side of the bungalow. To further save money, my grandfather tried to run the engine on paraffin, having first started and warmed it up on petrol. The result was a constant stream of break-downs which meant that my uncles' Sunday visit was often devoted to stripping down the various parts of the engine. They used to listen hopefully for its rhythmic sound while climbing Second Avenue. Silence meant trouble.

Beyond the living room was a largish entrance hall that doubled as an extra bedroom, with the official front door on the left. This was seldom opened, but gave access to a particularly attractive small porch area that faced south. You could sit here, elevated above the garden, surrounded by roses and hollyhocks. Turning right from the living room there was a small storeroom, full of cupboards and drawers that I was commanded to leave alone on pain of frightful retribution.

The bedroom at the front of the house proudly featured a large bay window, in the curve of which stood the bed with chamber pot beneath. To the left of the door stood my grandmother's treasured Spencer upright piano, on which she played almost every day, an accomplished self-taught musician. She possessed a large collection of sheet music reflecting her own personal tastes as well as the professional demands of a cinema pianist. My grandmother explained to me how she had had to choose music with the right mood to match sequences in silent films, 'Hearts and Flowers' or 'In a Persian Market' being typical examples.

Other departments of the sheet music collection added to the evocative pre-war atmosphere of the house, such as collections of 'Community Songs' with symbols 'for ukele accompaniment' from the world of the music hall and the days when a family party often involved a sing-song around the piano.

Opposite:
Family gathering, 'Wendover', Whitsun, 1958.

Opposite: Eddy and 'Pop' Forecast in the engine shed, 'Wendover', mid-1960s.

'Wendover', back garden, March 2010. Note the overgrown hedge at border with 'Vera-Joan'.

Stepping outside we'd see the toilet hut halfway down the garden. The original hut was a small affair but in the early '60s my grandfather replaced it with a far grander structure, at least six feet square with a proper tiled roof, two opening windows with net curtains and a battery-powered electric light with a jam-jar globe. Because of its unusual size, the new building became known in the family as 'The Arcade'. Behind The Arcade was a large enclosure serving as a coal store, big enough to take the entire winter's fuel, which could only be delivered in summer when the lanes were passable.

During the Second World War, an air-raid shelter was built behind the toilet shed, and this can still be seen today, forming a useful point of reference when working out where things were. From the mid-1950s it was used as a typical plotland 'useful wood and other materials' store. I remember it as being particularly dusty and unpleasant inside, hidden behind a large elderberry tree, generally neglected but with a flourishing loganberry bush planted on the earth roof. To the south of the shelter was the back lawn that extended to the vegetable patch and the rear fence.

In the 1950s when my memories of 'Wendover' began, my grandparents spent weekends and other more extended periods of time in their Dunton bungalow, the focus of a family gathering every Sunday. My Uncle Ed, Aunt Doris and cousins Graham and Keith would arrive with their motorcycle and sidecar from Upton Park, my Uncle Jack and Aunt Pauline from Chadwell Heath, also on a motorcycle. I would have travelled from Upton Park with my parents by train and stayed next door in 'Vera-Joan'. Harry Salmon would often be installed in 'Coombe Cottage'.

On such occasions, the lawns would be mown, ball games would be played and sometimes a large sun shelter would be pitched. Tea would be served in a scene duplicated many times

around the estate, followed by an early evening salad before everyone started back home to London. I would listen to my uncles, who were both managers of Co-op grocery shops, exchange news about the week's events and accounts of notable mechanical breakdowns and repairs.

The front garden at 'Wendover' had had the time to mature by the mid-'50s. The hawthorn hedge along the front was well established and neatly maintained. My grandfather had made a front gate himself with the name 'Wendover' in ornate lettering, set between two concrete posts, one of which still survives. Behind the hawthorn

hedge stood a tall poplar tree whose trunk extended up for some 10-12 feet and then split into two or three larger upright boughs, probably due to some pruning attempt in the past. This formed an ideal platform and I spent many hours up there, having an enhanced view across the flat landscape beyond the hill. The large pale trunk of this poplar can be seen at the present time, although it looks very much the worse for age.

Top left: The front garden of 'Wendover', 1966.

Above: Sidney and Rebecca Jackson in the front garden of 'Wendover'.

Behind the poplar was a large white snowball verbena bush. To the right, looking towards the bungalow, the hedge between 'Coombe Cottage' and the front garden consisted of several mature silver birch trees, one of which still survives, and a few other shrubs. The semi-circular front of the large bay window was planted with a red mass of valerian that attracted scores of butterflies in the summer. The front garden always looked at its best at that time, when the lawn had been freshly mown, sloping down towards the hawthorn hedge with the Hillcrest Avenue view beyond.

Walking was an unavoidable feature of plotland life. Every week after they had set up permanent residence in 'Wendover' in the late 1950s, my grandparents walked to Laindon to do their shopping, calling at our house in Shelley Avenue (off Berry Lane) on the way back for a cup of tea. This continued until they were over eighty years old, despite my grandfather's increasing knee problems.

They would spend Christmas Day with us. I would walk over to 'Wendover' early on Christmas Day and accompany them while they made their way along the paths, dressed in their Sunday best. We returned in the early evening, always grateful if there was a frost to freeze the mud in the stretch after the narrow concrete path ended.

Eventually, old age and health problems became insurmountable, and 'Wendover' was reluctantly sold to finance a move to Benfleet. They had to hire a tractor and trailer to move their belongings down the hill at a cost of £25. The bungalow that had been at the centre of our extended family life since the 1930s stood empty for a long time until it was finally demolished. Sapling trees were planted and the carefully tended lawns and hedges grew unchecked.

'Coombe Cottage'

When the Jacksons bought the land for 'Wendover', Harry Salmon purchased the plot next door, which he named 'Coombe Cottage'. Harry's bungalow, the successor to a shed at the rear of the property, had two rooms and a large roof space. The front door opened directly into the living room, but was seldom if ever used, being covered by a hanging blanket to keep out draughts. The back door opened directly into Harry's bedroom.

The front garden should have been a lawn, but since it was not cut regularly, the grass was always rather rough. Harry always justified this by claiming he liked to look at the wild flowers that sprang up, principally dandelions and daisies. Looking up from the large double gateway opposite the site of 'Hawthorn', a row of apple trees stood along the right-hand hedge. The bungalow stood on a levelled piece of ground that created a steep bank in the front, at least three feet in height, still visible in the new path that has now been cut across the plot beyond Hillcrest Avenue. Behind the bungalow, the level ground continued with steps up to the rear lawn. A slight depression can still be seen today on the site of this garden where a low retaining wall separated the higher level from the lower.

Below: The levelled front of 'Coombe Cottage'.

Bottom right: 'Coombe Cottage'.

If 'Wendover' gave the impression of being fossilised in the 1930s, Harry's bungalow gave the same impression of timelessness at least three decades before this. An educated man

and accountant by profession, Harry's hobby had been visiting second-hand bookshops and junk shops, acquiring anything that interested him. He had a large bookcase full of obscure books, many with ornate tooled spines. They all had small print and were way above my head, such as *Lord Chesterfield's Letters to his Son*, *Education: its meaning and purpose*, *Macauley's History of England* and so on. Harry was proud of his library and always encouraged me to take advantage of it, but with little success.

He took the *Listener* and *The Times*, which was printed in those days on far higher quality paper than the *Daily Mirror*, the *Daily Sketch* or the *Sunday Pictorial* that my family always read. Similarly, he had a battery radio, which, unaccountably to me, was permanently tuned to the Third Programme. When the piles of newspapers and magazines had grown too large, he would burn them in a magnificent bonfire at the end of his garden – and allow me to help. After moving to Dunton permanently, Harry channelled his literary interests into a part-time job, helping to run the newspaper and magazine stand on Laindon Station.

In his living room, he had a proper writing desk next to the window that overlooked the front lawn, with a typewriter and various pieces of office equipment. He could often be heard thumping away, typing letters or busy with his current project. I never knew what he was doing, although he had been involved in various publishing ventures in the past.

He had several large pictures on his walls, but the only one I remember was a black and white print of 'The Rokeby Venus' over the fireplace, which to me seemed strange and daring. An ancient pendulum clock mounted on the wall in a wooden case with weights on chains ticked seriously, completing the atmosphere of the room. There were photographs too, dating from continental tours to the Alps when he was a young man. A keen photographer, Harry possessed several cameras, using roll film and glass plate.

Harry's bedroom was Spartan, containing his single bed and the basic necessary furniture. Sometimes next to the bed there was also a ladder to the hatch that led to the roof space where Harry kept lengths of wood and other accessories for future use.

Directly behind the bungalow was a substantially built yet compact wooden shed that Harry used as a kitchen since he always said that he disliked the smell of cooking in the house. Here he had a single cold tap and a gas ring on which he would cook all his meals and then carry the food into the living room to eat. His preparation area was a small kitchen table just inside the door, surrounded by all manner of junk. A ladder led to the roof space where he kept more lengths of 'useful' wood in true plotland fashion.

Next to the kitchen was a storage shed made of curved corrugated iron with a wooden front and door, filled with more junk. Beyond

that was a large rectangular concrete tank sunk into the ground that was always full of water. I suspect that this was the base of a former Anderson shelter and may be viewed today to the east of the new path mentioned above.

Up a few steps to the higher level of the rear lawn and to the right was a small greenhouse, perfumed with geraniums. At the back of the property was a flagpole on which Harry would sometimes fly his large red ensign. In the far left corner of the plot stood Harry's small toilet shed, under a large oak tree that had formed part of an earlier field boundary. Harry rigged up a swing from one of its boughs, much appreciated by the Jackson children from next door. This oak tree is still to be seen, together with a row of concrete fence posts that extends along the rear of this plot and that of 'Wendover'.

For me as a boy, Harry was irresistibly interesting. I used to plague him regularly in our house in London and once he took me on an expedition to the Science Museum in South Kensington, with all its fantastic exhibits and working models. With three gateways and openings linking 'Coombe Cottage' to 'Wendover', I had free run of both properties as well as of 'Vera-Joan'. 'Uncle' was very patient and always put up with my constant visits, calling me 'The Earwig'.

Harry was a prime example of the plotland free spirit. His bungalow and sheds were totally different to anything I was used to at home and packed with all kinds of fascinating objects that he delighted in

Wallace Jackson and his sister, Becky, at the rear of 'Coombe Cottage'.

Harry in his hammock.

bringing out to show me, such as a nautical brass telescope, an old railway lantern with a large bullseye lens or a Victorian cast-iron stove case. He allowed me to help him around the plot. We sawed lengths of wood for fuel, increasingly available through negotiation as more and more plotland buildings were demolished. I had the opportunity to help him smash up a decrepit upright piano and a harmonium that he had decided were too far gone to repair and could best be used for firewood.

As the 1960s progressed, Harry's health declined and after a stroke he was taken to a care home. In the summer shortly before he died, his sister and her husband took me to visit him in their Jowett Javelin. It was very sad to see Harry, reduced by the stroke, a shadow of the intelligent and entertaining character he had always been for me.

The Area Today

Today the sites of these plots are part of the Langdon Reserve and are still identifiable – if you know where to look. The following map shows their locations in relation to the modern day paths on the Reserve.

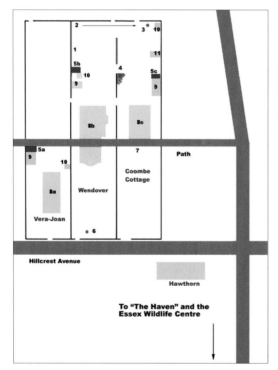

Plan of the three plots, 'Vera-Joan', 'Wendover' and 'Coombe Cottage', c.1960.

Key to the plan of the three plots:
1. Line of former hawthorn hedge
2. Line of concrete fence posts
3. Oak tree on former field boundary
4. Remains of former levelling of lawn
5. Anderson shelter
6. Tall poplar tree
7. Earth bank at front of levelled base for 'Coombe Cottage'
8. Bungalow
9. Shed
10. Toilet shed
11. Greenhouse

We shall now turn our attention to what it was like getting from London to the Dunton Hills Estate in the 1950s …

Chapter 5

The Walk From Laindon Station

This journey was a big part of the plotland experience for me as a small boy in the 1950s. These details are offered as a memorial to a vanished environment, my only apology being for any omissions.

The journey would start with a short walk to Upton Park station, through streets lined with terraced houses and well-maintained pavements on both sides. A District or Metropolitan train would take us to Barking station to join the main line to Shoeburyness from Fenchurch Street.

Getting on a larger train drawn by a steam engine seemed a rite of passage in itself to a small boy in those days. After what seemed an eternal period of waiting, its frightening, clanking, steaming, smoking explosion of an arrival underlined the start of an important event rather than a mere journey.

When the train pulled away, there was a sense of the power and purpose necessary to make the transformation from town, streets and traffic to open fields, fresh air and wide views. Past Upminster, where the underground trains could go no further, we entered the magic land and pulling out of West Horndon Station we prepared ourselves with some excitement for a glimpse of the hill, Dunton Colony and the Lower Dunton Road. Into the cutting, past the signal box and under the Durham Road bridge, and the train began to slow down.

Arriving at Laindon Station, we showed our tickets at the gateway to the left of the main station buildings. We turned left up the footbridge steps that led over three tracks to the High Road, at that point on a high embankment. From the footbridge we might still have been able to see the line of coach roofs of our train, headed by its steaming locomotive, or, if we were lucky, a London-bound train might be pulling away from the down platform with all the blasting sound, smoke and steam that was necessary in those days. If we were luckier still, there could be a through train making the whole footbridge shake with its speed and enveloping us all in aromatic smoke.

Having crossed the High Road, we went through the wicket gate to the wooden steps in two flights that led to a footpath alongside the railway land. From the top to the right you could see sidings and the railway cottages of Railway Approach on the other side of the railway lines. This side of the lines behind a wire fence was always overgrown with long grass. To the left of the steps, at the foot of the embankment, were trees and a deep ditch. Ahead, after leaving the civilisation of a row of bungalows along the cul-de-sac of Bristow Road, the path continued past an expanse of untamed bushes and more long grass.

This first stretch of the path was long and straight. Halfway along, if the line of bungalows on the left hadn't registered as being totally alien to the familiar lines of Edwardian and Victorian houses of East London, you now knew that you had arrived in a totally different world. Dog rose and brambles reached out from a wilderness of blackthorn and hawthorn thickets. A sharpish left-hand turn and the path continued to skirt the bushes on the left, leaving the railway on the right, now bordered by trees. Beyond this, just scrub and emptiness. Soon we reached a small bridge over a stream or large ditch, which on the left-hand side vanished into a mysterious swampy jungle of bushes from which you could sometimes hear the blurred sound of many birds. In winter this stream could be quite impressive, reducing to a trickle in the hottest days of summer.

An oblique turn to the left, then to the right, and we now had our first plotland unmade road on our right-hand side. After a 'crossroad' with grassy tracks leading left and right, we passed an increasing number of bungalows on the left. The path continued ahead to the left of a 'road' that was really just rough ground until it met Berry Lane at the junction with Bridge Road. Having emerged from the first section of plotland, we sometimes took advantage of the Victory Stores to buy supplies or an ice cream.

This shop, run by Mr and Mrs Lungley, was different to the general grocer's store I had known in Harold Road and a world away from the sophisticated shops in Green Street, Upton Park. You entered what looked like a converted bungalow up concrete steps and found yourself in front of a counter. Shelves of tins, boxes and packets filled all available spaces. A passageway to the right led further into the interior with another small counter on the left. A large shop window looked out, past a red pillar box across Berry Lane, to an expanse of trees and bushes.

Top: Electrification of railway in 1961/2, seen from Durham Road Bridge.

Centre: Berry Lane in the early 1960s.

Leaving the shop, we turned right into Berry Lane and found ourselves under oak trees on a road with a proper hard surface but no pavements. However, solid-looking houses and bungalows soon started to appear on both sides as the road began to climb a gentle slope. On the left, on the corner with Lincewood Park Drive, was another shop in a converted bungalow run by a Mr Cockshaw. Here you could buy Lyons ice cream.

Lincewood Park Drive, despite its grand name, was an unmade track that descended into trees and bushes, wet with ruts and oozing mud in winter. The corner of Shelley Avenue was graced with a large telegraph pole with a massive diagonal support. Unlike Lucas Avenue, wires were on display all along the lane. Still no pavement or consistent footpath, but occasionally a raised grass bank that just had to be walked along by small children.

After Shelley Avenue and Lincewood Park Drive, the slope became less gentle and we were glad to reach the top just past Shakespeare Avenue on the right and New Road that led down left to the recreation ground. In addition to bungalows, there were also houses. They all looked like well-established serious properties that had successfully controlled the wild country we had had a taste of earlier.

The end of the made-up section of Berry Lane had the atmosphere of border country. To the left, a track led to Great Berry Farm, or Markham's Farm as we called it. Ahead, with a row of dustbins forming a welcoming committee, the narrow concrete path that led to the Dunton Plotlands skirted the right-hand side of the old unmade Berry Lane that dipped between two fields, bordered by rows of towering elms. The dustbins divided the path from the lane, which always had deep ruts in its unmade clay surface; to the left was a row of tall elms, and to the right of the path was the open prospect of a field, usually planted with wheat.

Jim & Elsie Neale walking along Berry Lane path, early 1960s.

Having passed the bins, the path made a short chicane, roughly at the end of the first field, where another row of tall elms with a well-established rookery stretched off at a right angle to form a boundary. This was to skirt a ditch that appeared to the right of the path

From now on, the path was overarched by elms and in summer rampant nettle beds were a constant peril to bare arms and unprotected legs in shorts. To the left, the track became wetter in winter and the concrete path had been deliberately raised, almost giving the impression of a low causeway. In summer the grass grew lush and high with tall aromatic cow parsley.

Forest Glade in the 1960s.

Finally, we reached a T-junction. To the right, the original continuation of Berry Lane, now reduced to the width of a footpath between tall trees, led to Bridge Avenue, a bridge over the railway and Sumpners Farm Road. This path is still in existence today, running alongside a playing field for part of its route and named Hawthorn Path where it reaches Mandeville Way at its far end.

The main track continued to the left after the raised path sloped down to what could amount to a ford in the wettest winters. More tall elms made the stretch gloomy and cuckoo-pint flourished at the side of the path, with its red berries and distinctive green fleshy leaves. Finally the path emerged into light at the top of a slight rise to take a sharp 90-degree turn to the right. Here Forest Glade, or simply 'The Glade' as we called it, continued down a long slope. Resting on the corner, you had your first view of roofs and poplars in the Dunton Plotlands.

The Glade had been created by simply fencing off a strip of land to the north of two fields, which were now divided from the

concrete path by a barbed wire fence. I remember that in successive years these fields may have been put to cereals, wheat or barley, or provided grazing for cows. Once I watched a tractor up to its axles negotiating the deep mud in the lower field.

Halfway down the path, a ditch and tree-line marked the former field boundary. From this point onwards, the unmade grass track to the right became wetter in winter, the ruts deeper, and the mud more treacherous, sucking an unwitting boy's wellington boot down almost to the top. The deep, semi-liquid clay sometimes clung on so firmly when he tried to take a step forward that he would have to balance on one leg, trying desperately to avoid getting a wet sock, with the inevitable telling-off later. In summer, it could be a source of satisfaction to walk through the hard-baked deep ruts with impunity. In winter, the frozen mud created the same opportunities with the added advantage of ice.

To the north of the second section of The Glade, the tall elms gave way to low bushes and the first of the many patches of bramble that characterised the plotlands.

Plotlands

To the left was a field boundary and then a hedge around the first plotland property at the junction of Forest Glade with Beech Hall Gardens, a broad track covered in high grass. To the right, a raised path led across the unmade track, through bushes and low trees, to join the concrete path along the eastern side of Beech Hall Gardens. The path from The Glade now made a 90-degree turn to the left around a high hedge that made caution imperative, especially if someone was coming the other way on a bicycle.

The eastern side of the new track was now developed with plotland properties, mostly well-cared for, with neat lawns and

Bungalow on the corner of Beech Hall Gardens and Margaret Avenue, 1981.

paintwork, really living up to the name of the road. However, as the '50s merged into the '60s, the western side, across the long grass, had fewer buildings and looked more overgrown with bushes.

The first turning we reached was Margaret Avenue, a path through the grass that led off right, eventually reaching Hillcrest Avenue at the top of First Avenue. Sometimes we took that path for a change, past some high trees, after which the path switched to the other side of the track, past one of the few pine trees to be seen in the area, a property that contained a natural pond (which is still a feature of the landscape today) and some well-kept bungalows on the right, such as 'Eleanor'. At the top of First Avenue 'Everest' greeted us on

the right, but we would turn left into Hillcrest Avenue, admiring the view from the hill all the way to 'Wendover' or 'Vera-Joan'.

Members of the Neale family leaving 'Vera-Joan' on Hillcrest Avenue.

Normally, however, we continued along Beech Hall Gardens (passing properties such as 'Iris Villa') and turned right into Sunnyside Gardens, an increasingly ironic title as the years went by. Past a short outcrop of dog rose or brambles, and along towards a splendid white-rendered bungalow on the left, with low brick garden walls – Mr and Mrs Theobald's, as I remember. Shortly after that, the concrete path ended. You could either go straight on towards the top of Second Avenue through an opening in what must have been a former field boundary with several mature oak trees, or bear left through an overgrown area of long grass, dog rose, blackthorn and extensive brambles.

Paths and tracks led left to Ronald Avenue, or ahead to the rear of the properties 'Vera-Joan', 'Hillcrest' and 'Coombe Cottage'. In late summer, this whole area was the place to go for blackberries, some of which could be large and juicy, suggesting garden escapes of cultivated varieties. The blue-purple flowers of vetch could be seen among the long grass with the usual thistle and nettles. In winter, spring and autumn it could be very wet and muddy. In summer, grasshoppers and crickets sang in the heat.

Going through the rear garden gate of 'Wendover', you were immediately back in some sort of ordered world, with mown lawns, fruit trees, a carefully tended vegetable garden and, for no particular reason, sometimes a large red ensign flying from the flag pole in the adjoining garden of 'Coombe Cottage' if Harry Salmon was at home.

Next Deanna will look at the plots on the other side of the railway, whose residents probably made their journey from the station via Laindon High Road and Durham Road.

Chapter 6

The Plotlands to the West of Laindon

Little has been written about the plotlands in Laindon to the west of the High Road and north of the railway line, yet this was a well populated area. In this chapter we hear from plotlanders who lived there, and we take a look at some of their properties. The area was redeveloped by Basildon Development Corporation in the 1970s when it built the new Laindon West housing estates.

Individual plots of land were originally divided up and sold at land auctions and 'champagne sales'. The earliest began in the 1890s on what was called the Laindon Station Estate to the east of the High Road, and the land agent Thomas Helmore started developing his Manor Road estate to the west around 1903. A significant number of plots were bought by weekenders, many of whom eventually became permanent residents. As they had a longer period of time to become established, some of the properties looked quite substantial. One resident said she was told that the 'posh folk' lived on her side of the railway because they had more paths so didn't need to rely on their wellies as much. What a great way of defining plotland social status!

Helmore Crescent

Helmore Crescent ran parallel with the railway line and was a continuation of Durham Road. By 1949 there were around 30 properties in this road ranging in size from an estimated three to six rooms. Eight were wood with a corrugated iron or felt roof, and the remainder were described as being pebble-dashed, stucco or brick stucco.[1] Many of the plots had wells in the 1940s, although mains water was eventually laid – probably due to its proximity to Laindon High Road. Mains electricity later arrived via overhead wires and some residents took the opportunity to get connected during the 1950s or 1960s.

This was a road where many of the residents lived permanently. In 1942, Charles Leatherland's survey for the Dunton Parish Invasion Committee included data on 16 properties and showed that there were 64 people living in those properties at that time. Indeed, 11 were living in 'Carncastle' alone.

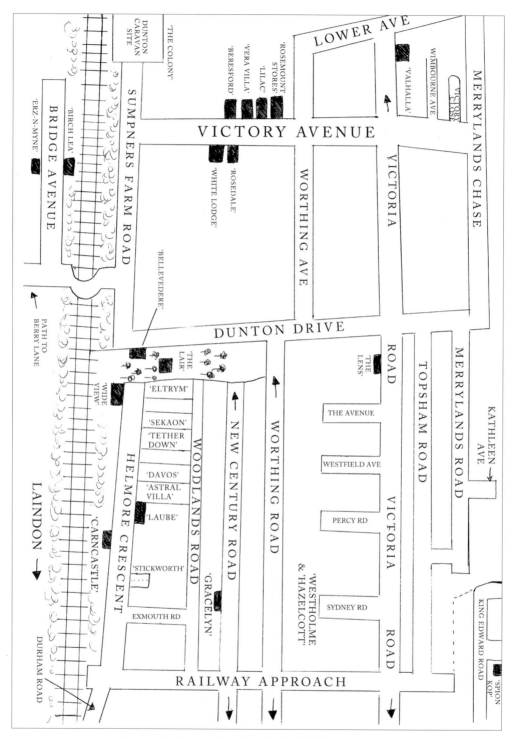

Lanes and plots mentioned in this book. Map not to scale.

'Stickworth' was one of the earliest properties to be built in the lane, appearing in a photo from 1900. This brick building stood in stark contrast to the many timber-framed buildings which sprang up in later years. By 1949 it was described as being semi-detached, probably having been divided, with 'Ameton' as its partner. Some of the early properties were originally built to house stable lads in the 1890s when there were proposals to construct a racecourse on land near the station. The plans came to nothing.[2]

Helmore Crescent ceased to exist in the late 1970s but the line of the lane is now roughly followed by Durham Road, which was extended in the 1970s. However, the name Helmores still exists in one of the side roads, roughly where the crescent would have finished at its Dunton end. Photos of the area in the 1960s and the present day are shown on p.173.

Let's hear from a couple of the residents who will tell us what life was like in Helmore Crescent.

Sheila Mountfort

Sheila Mountfort's parents, the Galpins, lived in 'Tetherdown' from the middle of the Second World War until their plot was eventually compulsorily purchased in the early 1970s.

Sheila said her grandfather and his brothers had bought plots in the area from 1900 onwards, and they were all Thames barge builders. Interestingly George Ross (another local resident) noted that many of the people who bought plots in this corner of Laindon were shipwrights from London, and he named 12 in New Century

Below right: 'Tetherdown' in 1969.

Below: Mr Davison in the long garden of 'Davos', *c.*1940s.

Road alone.[3] Clearly word of the delights of country living had spread among this group of workers.

Her grandfather's surname was Davison, so he named his plot 'Davos'. It was a large plot, having a frontage on both Helmore Crescent and Woodlands Road behind. In 1949 the survey described it as being a wooden building with a corrugated iron roof, estimated to have four rooms and judged to be in a fairly good condition.

Like many plotlanders her parents only came to live in Helmore Crescent when their own house in London was destroyed by a bomb during the war. They rented 'Tetherdown', a few plots down from 'Davos' and 'Astral Villa', which was owned by her great-uncle and his daughter. 'Tetherdown' was actually owned by the Simmonds family, who were corn merchants in Laindon High Road, but her parents eventually bought the plot from them.

'Tetherdown' was one of the larger properties in the lane. In 1949 it was estimated to have six rooms and was described as being pebble-dashed with an asbestos tile roof. Fortunately, as Sheila's family was living there at the time, the surveyor judged it to be in a good condition and said the plot was very well kept.

Sheila explains what it was like being a child in the plotlands:

> I would play with many of the local plotland children. We used to have to walk a long way on the unmade paths to Dunton School on Lower Dunton Road, often gathering more children en route. Often we would go to visit a plot at the corner of Dunton Drive near Helmore Crescent called 'Bellevedere' which was owned by the Day family. Mr Day was an old retired sea captain who had sailed clipper ships. He had built a model village in a greenhouse in his garden. The models were so detailed

'Bellevedere' in 1969.

> that the little butcher's shop even had joints in its window, and the baker's shop had buns.
>
> At the end of Helmore Crescent there was a narrow track where it joined Dunton Drive. This path was very dark as the neighbouring trees and bushes had grown together to create a thick canopy. Locally this was called 'The Spinney'. Once, my brother hung a luminous skull from a tree to scare people.

As mentioned earlier, Sheila's family owned a number of plots in the area. Sheila's great-uncle, Lionel Davison, was one of the last residents to leave and an active member of the Laindon Residents' Protection Association. When the Corporation wrote to him in 1975 to say his plot, 'Wideview', would be compulsorily purchased, Mr Davison refused to move and held out until 1978, when he finally had to relocate to Berry Lane.

I can remember a man, whom my parents called 'The Woodman', holding out against the Corporation and he seemed to be the last line of defence. This was Mr Davison. All these years I imagined he must have been some kind of lumberjack, but it turns out that he was a boat builder. He did indeed keep lots of wood weathering in his garden, but this was used for constructing the sailing craft.

Jeanne Sussex

Jeanne Sussex was another resident of Helmore Crescent in the 1950s when her family rented 'Laube' for a few years. 'Laube' was occupied by the Rugg family during the war, and in the 1949 survey it was described as being a three-roomed wooden building with a felt roof, and was judged to be in a fair condition. By the 1950s the felt roof had been replaced by corrugated iron. Compared with other plots in the road, 'Laube' was fairly basic and moving to such a seemingly remote rural location was quite a shock for Jeanne as she describes below:

I moved from Battersea in London with my parents, brother and sister in 1952. The house was opposite Battersea Dogs Home and had a tiny back yard. I was the eldest of us three. I was just fifteen and had just left school. My dad had the opportunity to rent a plotland property in Laindon. I think it was owned by some relations on my dad's side, and they are shown in the photo of 'Laube'.

I had just got a job in C & A in Oxford Street when my family moved there in June. Dad organised the move and my mother and I didn't even see it before we actually moved.

It was a real shock when we got off the train from Fenchurch Street and walked down the unmade roads along the railway into Helmore Crescent. We followed a path leading round from the station. The bungalow was situated right at the bottom of the land reached by a long winding path through an orchard of all sorts of fruit trees. I think we lost ourselves for a while in the orchard (and it wasn't long before we all ended up with upset tummies from over-indulging in fruit).

There was a small tap in the kitchen, but no bathroom or other plumbing. My dad had the job of emptying our outside loo etc. We had no heating, but my dad had a Parkray fire installed to suit the bungalow. Dad set about

The Rugg family at 'Laube', late 1940s.

improving the hut and filling in gaps in the wooden walls with newspaper so he could wallpaper over it.

At the time I didn't want to move from London as I missed my friends. My brother and sister still went to school at Laindon High Road Secondary so they got to know other children. I worked in Green's Stores in the High Road and later I trained as a GPO telephonist. We were only in our plotland home for about five years as my parents were offered a council house in Laindon, just off the High Road. But I'm glad to say it was the best thing dad did. I've realised since that this started my love of the countryside. I now belong to our conservation sites, and to Essex Wildlife Trust of course.

New Century Road

This was one of the roads running parallel with Helmore Crescent. In his book about the development of Basildon New Town and the work of the Laindon Residents' Protection Assocation, George Ross described how his family bought eight plots (half an acre of land) of former farmland in New Century Road in 1915 for the sum of £18 15s. 0d.[4] His grandfather bought some land next door. The Ross family used their plot, 'Gracelyn', at weekends until 1922 when they moved in permanently.

Ross described New Century Road as being about thirty feet wide. It started at Laindon High Road and was 'virtually a cul-de-sac about three quarters of a mile long ending in a spinney wood at Dunton End'. The lane was unmade, but eventually the plot owners clubbed together to pay for the materials and for a local man from neighbouring Woodlands Road to lay a flagstone path.[5]

In the early years, photos show the land to be very open with hardly any bushes or trees. There were few fences between properties. Those that did exist seemed to have been simple affairs made from small branches. Otherwise the division between the plots was simply pegged out. However, the plot owners gradually began to make their mark and began planting bushes and trees which changed the landscape and afforded more privacy.

Although many people still relied on paraffin and coal, Ross notes that gas was laid along the road in the late 1920s. Its proximity to the High Road probably helped New Century Road to get connected to the supply quicker than many other more remote plotland lanes. However, the poor state of the unmade road meant that there was often damage caused to the pipes and Ross notes that 'in the winter time, these leaking gas bubbles could be seen coming up through the puddles of water'.[6]

The self-built family bungalow, 'Gracelyn', was described in the 1949 survey as being pebble-dashed with an asbestos tile roof. It was estimated to have five rooms and judged to be in a fair condition. Overall the plot was described as being well kept. It was finally demolished by the Corporation in the 1970s and Merrylands County Primary School, in Cumberland Drive, was built on it.

Victoria Road

By the late 1930s Victoria Road had been extended and was almost a mile long, stretching from Laindon High Road almost to Lower Dunton Road. Ron Crafer, who moved to 'Florence Villa' when his family's home in West Ham was destroyed in 1940, explains that:

> It was intended to join both roads, but the owners of Dunton Colony would not sell, so the road had to stop short one field's width before reaching Lower Dunton Road. However, there was a right of way alongside this field known as the Cinder Track which led to the old school.

'Dunton Colony' mentioned above was on the site of Sumpner's Farm, which had been bought in 1904 by Joseph Fels and turned into a farm colony to train men from the workhouse in Poplar. The aim was to equip them with agricultural skills so they could make new lives for themselves overseas. It is now the site of Dunton residential caravan site.

Part of Victoria Road still exists, at the High Road end, but it has been severed by Southfields industrial estate at its western end.

Victoria Road at junction with Dunton Drive in 1960.

Rear of plots in Victoria Road in 1950s. 'The Lens' is marked. 'The Mecca' is to the left, 'Homeland' to the right.

Mr King at the back of 'The Lens'.

Roy King

Roy's family bought 'The Lens' in 1938 from Len Stubbs who had built the property. During the war the Kings moved permanently from Poplar and lived there until the 1960s. Roy remembers many family members sharing their home, including his maternal grandmother, Ada Rungay. She was a nurse and is mentioned in the minutes of the Dunton Parish Invasion Committee, which appear in our wartime chapter.

Merrylands Road and Topsham Road

These were neighbouring roads running parallel with Victoria Road towards the Dunton end. They were both unmade, but in 1949 the surveyor notes that at its very eastern end Merrylands Road had no path or road at all. Jean Dallinger gives her memories of living in both of these roads.

Jean Dallinger

My family were bombed out of Millwall and were first evacuated to Somerset. Around 1943 they came to live in a wooden bungalow called 'Eastville' belonging to my

dad's family in Merrylands Road. It had originally been
a weekend plot. It was set in half an acre of land which
enabled us to grow all our own vegetables and keep rabbits
and chickens. Water came from a well in the garden.

Although there was one shop and a Post Office fairly
nearby, we had to go into Laindon on a Friday to get the
rest of our shopping. Like most residents of these lanes,
we would use a wheelbarrow or an old pram to transport
our shopping along the muddy roads. It was quite a sight
to see all the folk from the plotlands trundling along the
High Road.

I married in 1954. I'd known my husband when we
were children as his family lived in 'Tanglewood' in
Topsham Road. He spent time in the air force and we
met up again when we were both working at Howard
Rotavators in West Hordon. Our first home was a
bungalow at the other end of Merrylands Road.

Having relatives nearby and intermarrying between plotland
families was very common. In many ways, the patterns of living
in London were simply transplanted into the countryside. For
Jean, proximity to her family was more important than having
better living conditions, as she explains below:

Workers at the Howard Rotavators were given the
chance to rent a new Corporation House in one of the
new estates at the other side of Basildon. We took up
this opportunity and moved. However, I missed being
close to my family and when I became pregnant with
my son we decided to move back. A bungalow called
'Homeleigh' was for sale in Topsham Road. It cost £850.
My aunt (who lived on a large plot called 'The Grange'
in Dunton Drive) lent us the money and we paid her
back regularly. Eventually we were bought out by the
Corporation. I actually worked for them for 20 years, as a
cashier in charge of taking rents and also a welfare officer.

Sidney Road
Sidney Road was a short, grassy lane off Victoria Road, and today
it would probably be under West Mayne or the houses of the
Presidents Estate.

David Blaine
David's parents lived in 'Westholme' in Sidney Road from the
1930s-'70s, and his grandparents, the Bradfords, lived opposite in
'Hazelcott'.

The Blaine family outside 'Hazelcott' in the 1940s.

Victory Avenue

Victory Avenue ran from the railway line northwards, cutting vertically through Worthing Avenue and Victoria Road. In 1949 it contained approximately 36 properties, estimated to have between two and five rooms. Sixteen were described as being wood or timber, 18 were stucco or pebble-dashed and two were brick. The majority of properties had asbestos tile roofs, but a couple had corrugated iron or felt roofs. A number were judged to be weekend properties, and there were quite a few plots described as being untidy.

David Blaine's mum and aunt in the garden in Sidney Road, 1930s.

We will hear now from Audrey Carter, whose family had a plot in Victory Avenue from the 1930s. Audrey is very keen to preserve the local plotland history. She is a volunteer guide at 'The Haven' museum and also organises an annual reunion of the Dunton plotlanders.

Audrey Carter

My memories of Dunton are very dear to me. I feel I had, in spite of the war and the hardships our parents endured, a privileged childhood enjoying the freedom that children today no longer have.

My parents were living in two rented rooms in Bow when I was born. My grandparents (the Flacks) were attracted to Dunton because of the advertisements in London of plots of land being sold. They would come for weekends and holidays, staying first of all in a bungalow in Wash Road, Laindon. This would have been around 1934, and then with relatives who owned a bungalow in Victory Avenue, Dunton.

In 1937 my grandfather was given a hundred pounds for selling a winning Irish Sweepstake ticket. This must have prompted him to put a deposit of £5 on 'Lilac',

Audrey Carter (right) and Isabella Flack feeding ducks at 'Beresford'.

Victory Avenue, that then became the family's holiday home until the outbreak of the war when they moved to Dunton permanently. The total cost was £165. How we all fitted into 'Lilac' I will never know. There must have been six adults and three children living in this small four-roomed bungalow, but somehow we managed. Eventually my aunts moved into their own bungalows in Victory Avenue leaving my mother, myself, my Uncle Ron and my parents in 'Lilac'.

Charles Leatherland's wartime survey listed 26 householders in Victory Avenue with 15 other plots named but with no data provided, although several were annotated as being empty or as weekend plots. He lists 96 people living in the road in 1942. The information about the Flack family of 'Lilac' shows there were six in the household. Unlike many of their

Audrey Carter and
her family in the
garden of 'Beresford'.

neighbours they appeared to be lacking a number of items on the
survey list, such as spades, shovels and picks. However, they did at
least have respirators, which were in good condition.[7]

> Quite some time after my grandfather died in 1942 my
> grandmother moved to 'Beresford' which was next door
> but one. I would often fall asleep in my bed in 'Lilac' and
> wake up the next morning in my grandmother's bed. This
> was possibly due to my Uncle Dick and my Uncle Arthur
> being home on leave.
>
> My Sunday school teacher also lived in Victory
> Avenue [Miss Cruchley of 'Rosedale']. Her father kept
> bees and when they swarmed he warned everyone to stay
> indoors. I can see him now walking down the avenue in
> his big beekeeper's hat.
>
> We even had a shop in Victory Avenue – a small
> grocery store run by the Drew family ['Rosemount
> Stores']. It was a strong focal point for neighbours to meet
> and put the world to rights. My friend and I used to buy
> Horlick's tablets to supplement our sweet ration!
>
> After the war the people who owned 'Beresford'
> wanted their bungalow back and my grandmother wanted
> to move back into 'Lilac', and we moved round the corner
> to 'Valhalla' in Victoria Road.

In the Corporation's 1949 survey Audrey's family's plots were
described as follows: 'Lilac' – three-roomed wooden building with
an asbestos tile roof in a 'fair' condition; 'Beresford' – three-roomed
brick building with an asbestos tile roof in a 'good' condition;

'Valhalla' – three-roomed timber building with an asbestos tile roof in a 'fair minus' condition.

> My grandmother died in 1955 and my Uncle Ron
> and Auntie Marion lived in 'Lilac' until 1962 when
> the properties were compulsorily purchased by the
> Corporation, thus ending our Dunton days. How fortunate
> we were to grow up surrounded by our extended family.
> We had to contend with unmade roads, getting water
> from a well or standpipe, no electricity and the toilet at
> the end of the garden but I wouldn't have swapped it
> for anything!

Now the area is under a new housing estate and an industrial estate, but Victory Avenue would probably have been roughly where the extension to Durham Road loops round to run parallel with Mandeville Way.

Next we turn our attention to Alexandra Road, on the northern fringe of this area.

Chapter 7

Life at 'Spion Kop'

Nina Humphrey lived in a plotland bungalow called 'Spion Kop' in Alexandra Road, which joined the unmade end of King Edward Road in Laindon. This part of the plotlands was divided up for sale around the turn of the century. 'Spion Kop' had no mains services, particularly in the early years, and her family were virtually self-sufficient. In the mid-1960s the modern town began to creep nearer and nearer to her family's home. A new housing development in Bourne Close arrived on their eastern boundary, and in 1967 Ford's Research Centre was built to the west of their property.

Nina described the life of a plotland child growing up in the 1950s and 1960s:

> 'Spion Kop' was my home for 23 years – 1946 to 1969, although it belonged to the family much longer than that, in fact from the First World War until 1975 when it was compulsorily purchased by Basildon Development Corporation. It stood in the corner of almost an acre of land at the far end of Alexandra Road. My memories start from around 1950, when the bungalow was made of wood and stood on low stilts.
>
> The property was first owned by my dad's mother, Amy Burton. My dad, George, was her youngest child, born in 1908. Amy was left the land and a wooden bungalow by James Burling when he died in 1915. He had bought the land from E. Wood in 1907 who, in turn, had bought it from the local land agent Thomas Helmore in 1904. At the time the bungalow was known as 'Honeysuckle Hall'.
>
> The family were living in Leytonstone, where they ran an antique/second-hand furniture business. Weekends were spent at Laindon, sometimes travelling there by horse and cart. Later, the bungalow was renamed 'Spion Kop' after the horse that won the 1920 Derby, influenced no doubt by the fact that Amy was a keen race goer.
>
> My dad met my mum, Jessica, in Laindon. She was the daughter of neighbours living close by in 'Pendennis'

in Alexandra Road. They married in 1930 and went to live at the Burtons' family home in Leytonstone. Following Amy's death in 1938 they decided to move to Laindon with my older brother, Dennis, and 'Spion Kop' became their permanent home.

Somehow, my dad managed to bring a London tram down to Laindon. He attached it to the bungalow, where it was used for extra sleeping quarters. The number '278' was still clearly visible on the front of the tram. I think its route might have served the Forest Gate and Stratford area. In 1975 when my parents moved, the tram was still standing in the garden. We suggested to my dad that it be offered to a museum for preservation. However, he didn't seem very interested and so it was left behind.

Over the course of several years my dad completely rebuilt the bungalow single-handed, and the tram was pulled away from the bungalow so I could use it as a playroom. He was a night worker so it helped enormously that he was around during the day. Sometimes he surprised us by painting the outside various colours. One time, he painted it white with a red trim. On arriving home from school my sister Anne exclaimed, 'Oh no, now we look like a post office.'

Burton family at 'Spion Kop' in 1920. Amy Burton is in the middle row, third from right.

George Burton with cousin outside tram in 1959.

Water

Our water was supplied from the collection tanks at the side of the house and was brought into the house in jugs and buckets. It was then heated on the stove. With no bathroom, a very large white butler sink was used for washing ourselves and our clothes. Baths were taken in a tin bath in front of a fire in one of the bedrooms. Babies and children were bathed in the sink. Our toilet was an Elsan in a garden privy.

My mother would do all the washing by hand in the butler sink with only a mangle to help with the drying,

which wasn't a problem in summer. Getting washing dry in the winter was a nightmare for her. I remember her hanging sheets out on the line, only to bring them in again because they had frozen into stiff boards. We only had a change of underclothes twice a week during winter because of the drying factor.

Many of the dwellings in our road had a well. In summer time the water level became very low and the Water Board would fill them from a large tanker which they parked in the top field. They unrolled their very long pipes and ran them from the tanker to each of the plots in turn, until all the wells were filled.

Around 1951 my dad decided we should have a well too and, with the help

Nina's brother, Alan, with former Anderson shelter housing generator, 1953.

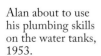

Alan about to use his plumbing skills on the water tanks, 1953.

of several pairs of hands, set upon digging out the hole until it was wide and deep enough. It then had to be lined with concrete, but first the small amount of water that lay at the bottom had to be removed. This was achieved by lowering me in a bucket on a rope, down into the dark well with my seaside bucket to scoop up the water. The well was a great success. My dad arranged for the Water Board to fill it regularly from a large tank on one of their vehicles. A water tank was installed in the loft and a pump fitted in the kitchen. Now we had running water in our kitchen. We used the system until Bourne Close was built at the boundary of our garden in the mid-1960s. We were then able to be connected to the main water supply and do away with the pump.

Energy

We used Calor Gas for lighting and cooking. The cylinders were stored under the sink in the kitchen. The mantles were white and soft and sometimes 'popped', went black and had to be replaced. I liked gaslight very much as it is soft and easy on the eye. It also flickered slightly if there was a draught.

In the early 1950s my parents bought a TV set from Squires in Laindon High Road. With no electricity, it meant having to run an electricity generator which was installed in an outside shed and ran on petrol. It had to be started by pulling on a rope which started the chug, chug, chug of the engine. That sound became very familiar in Alexandra Road as our neighbours also acquired their first TV sets. The system worked very well. We named our generator 'Jenny' and we knew when she was getting low on petrol because the picture would start to roll, faster and faster and then stop completely. Dad would dash to the shed and top her up and the picture would return to

'Spion Kop' having been remodelled, 1961.

normal. 'Jenny' did go wrong from time to time. On one occasion, my brother brought home a friend who was an absolute whiz with engines. He put all the pieces on newspaper that we had spread on the kitchen floor, located the problem and fixed it, much to our delight, and particularly that of my sister, who later married him.

In 1957 we were connected to the main supply electricity by overhead lines. Two young men did all the wiring in the bungalows and installed a trip box. If ever we used too much at one time, the system would trip and cut off our supply. We would have to turn off an appliance and then flick the switch on the box to resume power.

Heating

As 'Spion Kop' stood alone in the middle of an open field, it was extremely cold in the winter. Until the late '60s, our heating was coal and paraffin. A ton of coal would be delivered, tipped into our coal store and usually lasted us through the winter. Each room in the bungalow had a fireplace, although those in the bedrooms were rarely used. The kitchen fire was usually well underway in the mornings when we children got up, so we dressed and got ready for school there. When we arrived home from school, the fire in the living room would provide our heating, although we had to use curtains and draught excluders in various places. On very cold evenings, our bedrooms would be warmed with paraffin heaters. The coal fire would go out during the night and so we would heap more blankets and even coats onto our beds for extra warmth.

There were usually two or three chimney fires each winter in the neighbourhood. Smoke and sometimes flames would be noticed and the message would spread as to the location. We children would stop our games and run to the site and sit on the pavement opposite the house in question and listen for the bell of the fire engine and then watch while the firemen worked to put out the fire. Chimney sweeping was an annual event. Most households did their own. My dad had his own set of brushes and Mum would prepare the fireplace to catch the soot, while we children stood outside and yelled to Dad when the brushes could be seen coming out of the chimney pot. Our open fire was replaced with a Courtier Stove which had doors to the front. This meant that the fire kept until morning, making the bungalow warmer. The ashtray of the Courtier was also brilliant for roasting sweet chestnuts. During the mid-'60s, a Parkray was installed with a radiator in each room, finally providing central heating.

Refuse and Recycling

Refuse collections didn't extend into Alexandra Road because of the unmade road and therefore we had to dispose of our rubbish ourselves. Regular garden bonfires in summer and indoor coal fires in winter took care of most of it. Kitchen leftovers went on the compost heap. Some bottles were taken back to Pelham's shop in the High Street where we exchanged them for a few pennies. Other bottles and tin cans were collected and then taken to a communal waste bin on the corner of St Nicholas Lane.

One day it occurred to my parents that the disused well in the neighbouring derelict plot 'The Retreat' was potentially a future danger to anyone walking in that area and unaware of the large deep hole beneath. Therefore they decided to fill it in. We collected tins and bottles by the dozen and threw them down the well over a period of time, until it was full to the top. The well's cover was replaced and remains undisturbed to this day. It will provide a bit of history to anyone discovering it one day with its contents of Idris squash bottles and Campbell's soup cans, etc.

Old clothes, towels, blankets, etc. were put to one side and stored in a shed until there was a large pile. These were sorted into wool, cotton, etc., and taken to Turner's in Durham Road, where they would be weighed and we would receive a few shillings.

Food

We were virtually self sufficient for vegetables and fruit. We also kept chickens and goats. During the war years, as meat was rationed, my dad had kept rabbits too.

Mum would buy Rhode Island Red chicks by mail order which would arrive in cardboard boxes with punch holes in the sides. We also kept Khaki Campbell ducks and white Aylesbury ducks. My younger brother and I had fun with them. They had their own pen, where we dug a hole, sunk a tin bath and filled it with water. The ducks loved it.

We once had a pig that was kept in a sty near our oak tree. His name was Charley and he loved acorns. Eventually he was fattened up and taken to market, providing us with many pork meals over the following weeks.

We kept goats, which were a valuable commodity back then. A good nanny goat would provide one to two pints of milk each day for many years, and of course goat's milk

Nina's mum, Jessica, and her brother Dennis with hay sheds in background, 1934.

Nina (on right) with sister Anne and their goats, 1955.

doesn't have to be pasteurised. The baby goats were either kept or sold to new owners. We had a hay-shed with goat stalls attached where they slept at night. During the day they were tethered in the field alongside 'Spion Kop' where they helped to keep the grass short. They provided a couple of pints of milk each day and my dad became proficient at milking. I adored the baby goats and once they were able to start running around it was my job to keep them off my dad's vegetable patch. They were really playful and liked to run and jump for joy. They were very sure-footed and loved to climb, so I built them little towers and slopes out of planks of wood for them to climb and jump off.

I had not long started school when my parents got the first goat that I remember, 'Maisie'. She was either already pregnant or was mated soon after we got her, because she gave birth to twins. We named them Simon and Mary. Simon grew into a magnificent ram. He was what I would describe as an alpha male, leader of the pack, very large and powerfully strong. We had Simon for several years, but mum realised the danger that he presented and decided he would have to go.

It was almost impossible to sell a billy goat. We couldn't afford a vet's bill and we could never have got him down to the PDSA mobile van which parked outside the *Laindon Hotel*, so Mum decided to arrange for a marksman to do the job. We children were very upset.

We only kept a few goats at a time, and we gave some of the offspring to our neighbours. My parents finally had to get rid of our goats not long before they were forced to move due to the Compulsory Purchase Order in 1975. My mum was friendly with Mrs Franklin, who lived in 'Horton' in Alexandra Road, and gave her our two remaining goats, Mabel and Jill. One day Jill broke her tether and went running up Alexandra Road to 'Spion Kop' to be with Mum who was gardening at the time. It seems to me to be a sad little story that shows that goats don't forget their homes or owners.

One of our baby goats once got bitten by an adder. The poor little thing had a large swelling on its face and was staggering around in pain, almost unable to walk.

Thankfully after two or three days it began to recover. Adders were common in our garden and the neighbouring field. Many plotlanders will remember coming across them in their own lanes. They liked to sunbathe near hedges or patches of stinging nettles, somewhere they could retreat to if threatened. As children we were aware of the likely places we had to avoid.

During the war years my dad turned our garden into a smallholding with a large vegetable patch and fruit trees including many varieties of apples, Victoria plums and greengages. Soft fruit bushes included black and redcurrants, gooseberries and loganberries. In summer, one particular redcurrant bush in the front garden was alive with bees swarming and buzzing around it.

One summer when we had a bumper crop of fruit my sister and I were able to sell our surplus. My mother filled paper bags with 1lb of plums, greengages, etc. We walked along Devonshire Road and its adjoining roads, knocking at doors and offering the bags of fruit for a few pennies a lb. We sold lots and made several shillings.

Neither Mum nor Dad were particularly good cooks. Meals were basic and so long as our appetites were satisfied, it didn't seem to matter how the food looked or tasted. Flavouring with herbs or spices never happened. The most exotic thing we had was home-made mint sauce when we had lamb. We got it from 'The Retreat's' old herb garden. Today, chives still grow prolifically in the grassland on the site.

Other provisions had to be bought from the shops in Laindon. With no fridges or freezers to keep food fresh, shopping for meals was almost a daily chore. A 'safe' was the nearest thing we had to a fridge – a box with an open front covered in mesh to keep the flies away.

The large vegetable patch in February 1975. Ford's Research Centre can be seen in the background.

Hunting

Life during the war and the years following saw a lot of hunting in Laindon. Most households owned a gun. In fact we had a shotgun that stood in a corner of our kitchen behind where we hung our coats. Hunting trips were quite commonplace in Laindon. I remember an occasion when I was about five years old. A neighbour took a group of half a dozen of us children hunting with him. We followed along behind him over several fields, where Ford's of Dunton is now sited, with his eager springer spaniel at his heels and his shotgun over his shoulder. On that occasion nothing was shot, but the same neighbour often had pheasants and rabbits hanging in his scullery. The sound of gunshot firing was not unusual in our area so we didn't think much about it.

When I was about 12, while flying my kite in the field alongside 'Spion Kop', I suddenly felt a whoosh of something rushing past my head and shoulders and a sting on my arm. I was momentarily puzzled, but quickly realised I had been shot. Our neighbour, probably while shooting at wood pigeons, fired a shot through the hedge of the field and hit me. I ran in to tell my mum. Obviously extremely alarmed, she paid a visit to the neighbour, who later came to our house and sincerely apologised. His gun was a 12-bore spread shot and it is amazing that I wasn't severely injured.

A Worker's Life

Like many plotlanders Nina's father worked in London and made the regular commute by train from the backwoods to the capital every day. It must have been a strange experience, leaving behind the wellies and wells and entering the 'hi-tech' environment where he worked. Nina gives a child's-eye view of this daily ritual:

My dad did permanent night work. He was a Night Supervisor of the International Telephone Exchange when it was part of the GPO. He was based at Faraday House, near St Paul's Cathedral, but covered various other exchanges in London and Essex. He always left the house at 5 p.m. and marched all the way to Laindon Station. I would watch from the living room window as he walked down our path, turning every few yards to wave to me. As he turned from Alexandra Road into King Edward Road, I watched his progress through gaps in the hedge. About half an hour later, I would see the smoke from the train as it pulled into Laindon Station, and watch it on the horizon as it pulled into West Horndon, and then made its way to London, the smoke rising high into the clouds and finally drifting away. When I awoke the following morning, he was already home from work. It was his shift work pattern that allowed him the time to work on the bungalow and garden.

One day when playing in a friend's garden, we saw my dad going off to work. My friend's mum said, 'I see him this time every day marching along with his raincoat over

George Burton
at work – at the
International
Telephone Exchange
in the 1950s.

George Burton at
home – haymaking
on Coopers' field.
1958.

his arm – is he a detective?' I later discovered
that my friend thought that our home was
called 'Spy and Cop'. Maybe that is why she
thought my dad was a detective.

A Plotland Childhood

I adored living at 'Spion Kop' but I wasn't
aware that my home was different in any way
until I started school. Most of my classmates
at Markhams Chase School [now called Janet
Duke School] lived in council houses on the
King Edward Estate and the prefabs along
Railway Approach. I would play after school
in Devonshire Road with school friends, who
were curious as to where I disappeared to
along the unmade road when going home. One
afternoon I offered to show them where I lived.
They followed me along the boards which
turned right into Alexandra Road leading
to our gate at the end. There I stopped and
pointed up the path to 'Spion Kop'. My little
companions stood looking in silence for a few minutes
until one unpleasant little boy said, 'I wouldn't like to live
in an old cookhouse like that.'

I was very proud of where I lived, so his remark set me
back momentarily, but I wasn't fazed for long. I realised that
although their homes were more attractive and had more
amenities, they had tiny gardens. Mine had an enormous
garden surrounded by wide open spaces and farmland

and I wouldn't have swapped with any of them. This was confirmed when, after having given me a lift home in her car when I had been unwell at school, a teacher announced to my classmates the next day that she had had the pleasure of seeing where I lived and said that Nina lived over 'fields and fields'. I glowed with pride.

We didn't go away for holidays because we didn't need to. Our garden had a swing and seesaw made by my dad, a sand pit, a play room (the tram), my favourite oak tree to climb and the pond to go fishing in. We did, however, have occasional days out like taking the train down to Southend to play on the beach and in Peter Pan's Playground.

When Nina got into her teens she discovered the delights of the local entertainment scene. She would often go to the Mecca, which is where she met her future husband, Colin. She happened to mention that her portable record player was broken and he volunteered to fix it. A few days later he dutifully arrived, and found himself entering a strange plotland world. At the time, Nina's dad was in the middle of fixing a hole in one of the bungalow's walls, using scrunched up newspaper and chicken wire, and when Colin wanted to use the toilet he was handed a torch and sent outside into the middle of nowhere. Then, on his way home, carrying the record player in a vanity case, he was stopped by the police as they thought he'd stolen it. It's amazing she ever saw him again!

The simple pleasures of plotland life often lost their attraction for many teenagers, who wanted the excitement offered by 'modern life'. However, Nina says she never lost her love of this life.

Alan in garden of 'Spion Kop' in 1964. Note how the lawn shows signs of former ploughing furrows.

I was very much an outdoor girl. I loved the garden and surrounding fields, the fresh air and freedom of it all. I started my first job a few days after my 16th birthday (in 1962) and although I enjoyed it, I found it very hard to adjust to an office environment with just two weeks' holiday per year. I craved for my slowly disappearing childhood. The first winter at work seemed particularly long and dark. Walking the unlit boards on the way home wasn't pleasant, as once I had left King Edward Road it felt as if I were wearing a blindfold. However, I knew every inch of the way in the pitch black and was never afraid of the dark outside.

I well remember one winter's day when there had been continuous heavy rain. Upon arriving at the start of the boards on my way home from work, I was confronted with a river. The water was several inches deep, flowing quickly and it was still pouring heavily. I hesitated and then made the decision not to ruin my shoes. I took them off and waded all the way home barefoot in cold muddy water.

As the winter turned to spring, I was so looking forward to the four-day break at Easter. I awoke very early on Good Friday morning before anybody else. I was delighted to see that a beautiful day had dawned and I just had to get out there. Without changing out of my nightdress (a rather glamorous long yellow floaty gown of layered nylon purchased from Littlewoods in Basildon) I went into the garden. I started walking down the path towards where my grandparents' plot 'Pendennis' had stood. I floated along, feeling a bit like a film star in a long creation. I continued down Alexandra Road in the early morning sunshine.

Great tits and chaffinches were calling to each other in the hedgerow at the start of the nesting season. There was a buzz in the air that can only be experienced in a country lane. I felt as if I were in heaven. I was the only person around. The rest of the world was still asleep. I then realised that people would soon be waking and, alarmed that I might be spotted in my nightdress and thought to be some strange, mad female, I headed back to 'Spion Kop'.

The memory of that early morning walk is one of my very favourites. If ever I feel a bit stressed, it is the happy place in my head that I float off to – and it works every time.

Chapter 8

Back to the 1950s
A Walking Tour of Alexandra Road

We are about to step back in time to the 1950s and take a summer-time walking tour of the Alexandra Road area, based on the 1949 survey data and Nina Humphrey's memories. Laindon residents who live near King Edward Road, or those who enjoy wandering through Victoria Park, may not even realise that these locations were formerly the site of plotland homes.

Our walk along the former Alexandra Road and the stretch of King Edward Road up to the junction with Devonshire Road will be on muddy unmade roads. Summers in the past were not always as dry, hot and sunny as they are often remembered. In fact many of the Essex summers in the 1950s were dismal. In its annual report, Basildon Development Corporation even noted that the summer of 1958 had been the wettest on record, which caused many problems with its building programme.[1]

So let us now roll back the years …

Back to the 1950s
Unfortunately it has been drizzling all morning. The recent wet weather has left the unmade road in a poor state. Therefore you might want to leave your pair of winkle-picker shoes at Nina's house and don your wellies. Don't worry if they don't match what you are wearing. Young Nina understands this tricky fashion issue all too well, as she explains:

> Because of the state of Alexandra Road, particularly in winter, shoes are always a problem. I have to wear 'sensible' stout tie-up walking shoes which I think of as boys' shoes. I hate them and would prefer a more feminine style with a strap and buckle. When I get older I'm going to buy my own and carry a spare pair to change into.

We'll start our tour in the grounds of 'Spion Kop', sitting in its acre of land at the very end of Alexandra Road, surrounded by fields. In the 1949 survey 'Spion Kop' was described as being 'a three-roomed timber sheet building with an iron roof'. Rather

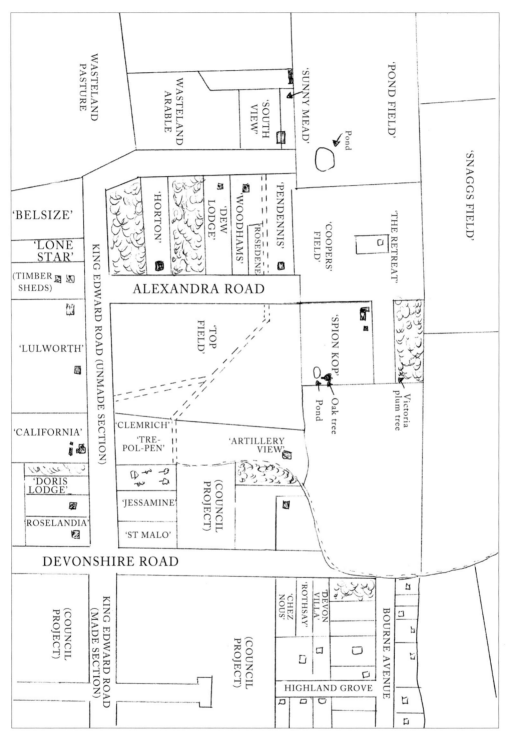

Map showing the area we are touring in the 1950s.

Border of 'Spion Kop's' garden. Telegraph poles mark the start of Alexandra Road.

unflatteringly it was judged to be in poor condition, but it looks quite different now as Nina's dad has recently remodelled it. The bungalow sits in the top left-hand corner as you look at the plot from Alexandra Road. It has been extended by the addition of an old London tram which has been attached to one side. At the rear of the bungalow sits the old Anderson shelter which now houses the generator, and next to it you will see the outside loo. There is just time for a quick visit before we start our walk.

Behind the bungalow you can see a hedge which separates 'Spion Kop' from the neighbouring field. In the middle stands a fantastic Victoria plum tree which is loaded with fruit. Nina points towards it.

> As you can imagine, it is a great favourite with local children who often come scrumping. Look up into the tree. Can you see what appears to be a large dog kennel wedged into its branches? My brother and his friends built this tree house, and goodness knows how they hauled the dog kennel up there. They even have a doorbell fitted at the bottom of the tree for visitors to buzz! There is no point buzzing, as I can see there is no-one at home.

Nina begins to lead us down the lawn. An herbaceous border stretches alongside the hedge boundary on the right-hand side. On the left-hand side of the lawn we can see Nina's father working on his vegetable patch using his new Bantam Rotovator. The noise of the petrol-driven machine stops as he turns it off and waves as we pass.

A pond can be seen at the end of the garden, near an old oak tree which Nina used to climb with her sister:

Our oak tree is very special and dear to us. It is easy to climb and the branches at the top form a sort of seat. I once sat at the top with a classmate playing our school recorders. My sister Anne and I spend a lot of time climbing that tree. Can you see the two lower parallel branches? That's where I normally hang upside down from. I would demonstrate, but we are a bit pushed for time.

As we exit the garden by a gate onto Alexandra Road I will let Nina guide us for the rest of the walk. She explains what we can see around us:

Nina's nephew, Paul, and Alan Burton, with 'The Retreat' in the background.

The fields on the west and north sides of our plot form part of an L-shaped piece of ground where a bungalow called 'The Retreat' now stands empty. It had been the home of the Cooper brothers, known as Old Fred and Old Jim. Fred was married with a daughter and Jim was single. They are all dead now and the brick bungalow has stood empty for years, slowly deteriorating. The land was overgrown and derelict even when it was surveyed in 1949, yet the garden had once been well cared for. Sometimes my sister, Anne, and I venture into 'The Retreat'. Originally it must have been quite a 'posh' dwelling as it has a very ornate fireplace in the living room and a harpsichord against one wall that still plays. We often run our fingers along the keys to hear the distinctive sound. My mum worries that the building might collapse so I won't take you there today.

The Coopers led a reclusive life, and apparently Fred's lonely daughter once convinced her parents that she had been proposed to by a pilot who landed in a nearby field. The story goes that they even bought a wedding dress.

Sadly most of his family had died by the 1940s and Jim Cooper went to lodge with our Nan in 'Pendennis', until he eventually went into a home in the mid-1940s. Since then, 'The Retreat' has lain empty, slowly deteriorating while my dad tends the land. The land would have turned to scrub but for his efforts.

We tether our goats on 'Coopers' field' but keep one large area of meadow to grow hay which we cut in August. I love this meadow and the beautiful wild flowers that grow there, including marguerites, vetch, poppies and common spotted orchids. Last month, my dad cut the grass as we needed the hay for winter feed for our goats. It was hard work, but my dad enjoyed doing it. He used to use a scythe which he wore attached to a harness over his shoulder. However, recently he bought a petrol-driven cutter which makes the job much quicker and easier. We all pitch in when we can. Sometimes Dad cuts the grass and then has to leave us to it, while he goes to work. We rake the hay into heaps, pile it on a large tarpaulin sheet, drag it to the hay shed, then throw it in and climb on top to flatten it down. It is always a relief once it is done, just in case it rains and gets spoiled. I'm glad we finished the task before this recent patch of wet weather set in.

The Coopers' land is surrounded on all sides by fields, each having a name: The Pond Field, Snaggs, Buckingham's Field and The Top Field. On fine Sunday afternoons, after our roast dinner, we sometimes take a walk to the 'slopes'. This means cutting through the hedge in Cooper's field and walking across to the far side of 'Snaggs'. This is a dome-shaped field and we children love climbing to the top and running back down again. A hedge separates 'Snaggs' from the next field, which leads to the Arterial Road, the A127. There are high grassy banks at the side of the road and we sit at the top and watch the cars travelling back and forth from London to Southend.

The Burtons haymaking on Coopers' field next to 'Spion Kop', 1964.

Leaving 'Spion Kop' and the Coopers' land behind us we can now take a stroll down Alexandra Road. This section of the road is known locally as 'The Boards'. Wooden sleepers were put down to form a solid footpath for us to walk along in the winter. Running alongside 'The Boards' is a track that can take a car, but only during the summer. The wooden boards regularly deteriorate and various methods are used to improve it. Just ahead is one particular boggy place which has been filled with a heap of winkle shells. You can feel them crackling underfoot as we walk on them. Around 1950/1, all the men who lived in Alexandra Road got together and remade the road with a consignment of shale, which they spread and smoothed out very successfully. It was a great improvement for a while, but a couple of brothers who lived 'down the farm' rode their motorbikes regularly along the road and made a mess of it.

On the left you can see the 'Top Field' behind the hedge. On the opposite side of Alexandra Road are a number of plotland bungalows. The very first bungalow we reach on the right-hand side is 'Pendennis'. This is owned by my mum Jessica's parents. The surveyors had described 'Pendennis' as a 'two-roomed stucco building in a fair condition with a corrugated iron roof'. It is still wooden, with the outside rendered with pebble-dashing which has been whitewashed. But it's now got a slate roof. The estimated size was slightly wrong as it has two main rooms, two small bedrooms and a 'scullery' which is used as the kitchen.

My mum moved from Bethnal Green to Laindon with her family in the spring of 1923 shortly before her ninth birthday. The family lodged at the Farm House while 'Pendennis' was being built. My grandfather, Henry Devine, who we called 'Nanpa', initially found it very difficult to find work and at one point my nan was considering moving the family back to Bethnal Green so that Nanpa could go back to his old job at the Glaxo baby food factory. However, after watching the children playing in the field outside in the sunshine, Nan decided she couldn't possibly take them back to London.

Eventually, Nanpa joined the GPO and worked as a postman for 25 years. It meant an extremely early start, as his round covered Laindon and Langdon Hills, including calling in at the TB Sanatorium off Dry Street, finally arriving home mid-morning. Interestingly, Nanpa and his father sometimes went by the name Richard Gardner.

My grandparents won't mind us calling in (but wipe your feet first) so let's go inside. The main living room has a table and chairs, a couple of armchairs and a large black put-you-up bed settee with a horse hair mattress. It is actually hard and uncomfortable – like sitting on a wooden box.

Nina's nan, Jessica Devine, at 'Pendennis' in 1950.

On one wall there is a large framed photograph of Nanpa aged 22 in his army uniform. On the opposite wall is a certificate from the GPO for his 25 years' service and a photograph of their son, Harry, who died from polio in May 1928, aged eight. Nanpa's radio sits on the table where he listens to football matches. On the side of the speaker is a row of collectable Robinson's Jam gollies.

Above the fireplace is the mantle shelf complete with a box of 'spills'. I enjoy helping Nanpa to make the spills, which are tightly rolled up pieces of newspaper for use when lighting the fire. Within the hearth there is the usual coal bucket and a set of tools, tongs, shovel and poker. On each corner of the front of the hearth sits a brightly painted gnome. Nan once told me she had bought them from prisoners of war who worked on the Southend Arterial Road. They made such ornaments to sell in order to make a little money.

At the rear of the bungalow is a long garden with a large vegetable plot, tended by my grandparents. However, some food grows all by itself. One autumn we had a bumper crop of large field mushrooms growing in the hedge between Nanpa's garden and Cooper's field. Some were as big as dinner plates and one alone filled the frying pan. Mum fried them in butter and they were delicious.

When I was very young, Nanpa had a horse and trap which he kept in the back garden. I remember being taken out in the trap to visit an uncle who lived in Billericay. It was wonderful sitting in the trap with Nanpa driving, and Billy, the horse, trotting along the roads.

As we head to the front gate I can hear my grandparents pottering around. If you listen you can hear

Nina (on left) and cousin Joan in the back garden of 'Pendennis'. 'Rosedene' can be seen next door.

Nan humming to herself as she goes about her chores and Nanpa is reciting one of his favourite poems. We can hear the odd line as he picks some vegetables in the garden: 'Half a league onward … rode the six hundred'.

My grandparents may not be able to live here much longer due to Nanpa's health. He suffers from chronic bronchitis. Recently he had bronchial pneumonia and had to be taken to hospital. The unmade road created great difficulty for the ambulance driver, so Nan is reluctantly making plans to move.

As we turn right out of 'Pendennis', the next bungalow is 'Rosedene'. Both bungalows are set at the front of their plots and have long back gardens. 'Rosedene' is what the surveyors called 'a stucco building with two rooms and an asbestos tile roof'. It is owned by Thomas and Rose Whitehead. They have four children, including twins who are only two years younger than me. They've held several birthday parties in the Top Field opposite, which are always good fun. They too are planning to move from the area, to the Lee Chapel North area of Basildon.

There is a rough track in between the two bungalows that leads to the far end of 'Rosedene's' back garden. A gate leads to a brick farmhouse which was previously owned by the Richards family who used to farm the land. They moved to 'Sunnymead' from Bethnal Green in 1919, and ran a milk delivery business from the farmhouse until the 1940s. Their horse and cart was apparently a common sight in the area.

Incidentally, Rose Whitehead from 'Rosedene' was one of the Richards' daughters, so she didn't move too

The Richards from Sunnymead Farm, 1920s. 'Pendennis' can be seen in background.

far when she married. By the late 1940s the Richards had left the farmhouse and it was turned into a two-storey semi-detached house and rented out. However, we still always refer to the buildings as 'down the farm'. One house is still named 'Sunnymead'. The Thompson family live there with their two sons who are around my age. Mrs Thompson is called Ruby and she is always dashing around in a hurry. There are other people who also live there at the moment, a grandmother and a couple of men who live with the family – MacDonald, who is a tall and suave-looking gentleman, and Arnold, who I believe is a farm worker.

'Sunnymead's' semi-detached partner is named 'Southview'. It's a brick building covered with stucco and has a slate roof. It's got about six rooms. It has been rented out to a number of families. At one time the Parker family lived there with two lads who rode their motorbikes up and down Alexandra Road and spoiled the shale path. The Mitchell family lived there for a while, and then the Jones family – but they have just moved to Basildon. I used to play with their children, so I miss their company. My sister also recalls roller skating in a cow shed on the land.

We won't bother taking a detour to try to recreate my sister's roller-skating antics, and will continue down Alexandra Road, passing some more plots that are owned by members of my family. The next on the right is called 'Woodhams'. As you can see, it's a timber building with an asbestos tile roof. It has a couple of rooms, but it is unusual because the building is in two sections. The living area is at the front and the sleeping section is a few yards behind. It was owned by Charles and Lizzy Jones. Lizzy was a friend of my Nan's and they have recently been rehoused on the King Edward Estate.

The next plot is 'Dewlodge', which is a two-roomed bungalow covered with stucco and has a slate roof. It is owned by William and Daisy Hughes. Daisy is the sister of my relative, William Peall, who lived in the nearby 'Horton'. Both 'Woodhams 'and 'Dewlodge' are set further back from the road, with most of the garden being at the front.

Passing a clump of bushes we next reach 'Horton' where Nanpa's older half-sister, Emily, used to live with her large family. She and her husband, William Peall, had nine children in all (eight boys and one girl). I am not sure who moved to Laindon first, Nanpa or his half-sister. One of Emily's granddaughters (Irene) and I were classmates at school when we were sixteen. The surveyors called 'Horton' 'a stucco brick building in a poor condition with four rooms and a slate roof'. Cheek! You can see that it has a large frontage and the building is close to the front fence. We pass very close by as we walk along the boards.

When Emily died in the mid-'50s a nice middle-aged couple called Mr and Mrs Franklin moved in. Mr Franklin works at Howard Rotavators in Horndon, and they own two very smart Daimler classic cars.

Afternoon tea at 'Pendennis' in 1950s. Minnie Thorpe on left; Nina's nan Jessica in middle; family friend on right.

We are now reaching the end of Alexandra Road. King Edward Road runs across the top of it. There are only a couple of plots on the right-hand side of King Edward Road opposite the entrance to Alexandra Road. The one on the right is called 'Belsize' and is owned by Mr Hadley. It's a timber building with around three rooms and an asbestos tile roof. The other timber bungalow with the asbestos tile roof is 'Lone Star', which is owned by Harold and Minnie Thorpe. It's small, and the surveyors thought it only had one room.

Directly opposite there are a number of timber sheds belonging to 'Lulworth'. This is the first bungalow we reach as we turn sharp left into King Edward Road. It's a three-roomed building coated with stucco and has an asbestos tile roof. Mrs Nellie Travers lives here so we refer to her bungalow as 'Traverses'. She is a small, elderly widow who rarely goes out. She speaks beautifully, which makes me think of her as rather 'well to do'.

Gentle-mannered, with a soft voice, Mrs Travers sometimes likes to borrow my mum's Kays catalogue and place a small order. On these occasions, I have to deliver her purchase and collect the payment. I dread this task because of her collection of dozens of Toby jugs which scare me rigid. I hate the things. Each has a gargoyle of a face which seems to leer down at me from the shelves. She leaves me standing at the door with all those ugly faces, while she disappears into the dimly lit bungalow to get her purse. My feet are always cemented to the spot while I endure a few minutes of lonely terror watching those bulging eyes and crooked grins. Such is my relief when she eventually returns and counts the shillings into my hand that I say a quick 'thank you', turn tail and run all the way back to the safety of 'Spion Kop' without stopping. Thankfully we don't have to deliver anything from the catalogue today.

Mrs Travers once ordered a pair of white silk, elbow-length gloves. I arrived at her bungalow with them and knocked on the back door, which was the entrance to her scullery. Mrs Travers came slowly to the door and smiled gently at me, then took her time to try on the gloves and examine her purchase. She slowly eased her fingers into the gloves and then rolled the long sleeves up to her elbows, smoothing them carefully. She held up her white silk-clad arms, admired them for a few moments and then with a satisfied smile said, 'Yes, they will be fine'. I stood there wondering where and when she would ever wear such an article of fine clothing, then decided maybe she just liked owning them.

Let's move on. Can you hear a man singing? I think it must be one of our regular postmen – 'Bing'. He's a very jolly, red-faced man who is always singing Bing Crosby songs – hence his nick-name. Yes, there he is just leaving the neighbouring plot, 'California', and heading away from us. Our other regular postie is a man who Nanpa worked with in his post office days, known as Waggy Lambert. He comes from Billericay. When he makes his round he free-wheels his bike across the top field, with his legs sticking out at either side, his post bag slung over his shoulder, bumping along very fast. I often wonder how he manages not to go flying over the handle bars. It's lucky he isn't delivering today as he'd certainly find it hard to ride across the muddy field.

Nanpa in his GPO work clothes.

There are several more bungalows before reaching the junction with Devonshire Road, which is where the made-up part of King Edward Road begins. The largest is the next on the right which is called 'California'. In 1949 it was described as being 'a four-roomed brick stucco building with slate roof and was in a good condition'. At that time the occupants were Charles and Lily Schofield and George and Rene Soper. However, by the 1950s a family named Bird had moved in. When I was about four years old, I sometimes played with their youngest son, Jimmy, and we had fun riding our three-wheel bikes together. There are rumours that 'California' is about to be sold and turned into a pig farm.

I didn't really know Mr Bird, but apparently he was a rather 'larger than life' character who owned an American Ford Thunderbird car that he kept parked by the side of the bungalow. Unfortunately he was killed when his car hit the kerb and turned over on the A127 while he was driving back from London. The accident was reported in the *Laindon Recorder*.

We sometimes have to collect our milk from 'California', when the unmade road is too wet and muddy for the milkman to attempt delivery. Mrs Bird has a rather excitable Yorkshire terrier, who she struggles to keep under control while she fetches the milk. She also has a large ferocious Alsatian called Rex which belonged to her husband. It is notorious as it terrorises everyone when it is allowed out to roam the neighbourhood. When this happens, every household panics, dashes inside and puts up the shutters so to speak, because that dog is so feared. It only takes one person to notice that Rex is out, raise the alarm and the word spreads quickly. Small children start screaming and are quickly gathered up by the adults. My mum will shout, 'Come inside quick! Rex is out!' We have to stay inside and watch from behind the curtains while Rex menacingly patrols 'The Boards', snarling and threatening anything or anybody in his way.

Don't worry – I think Rex must be tied up in the back garden at the moment because 'Bing' was still singing happily enough when he finished delivering post. However, we will have to keep an eye out when we walk by.

There is a small patch of wasteland next to 'California' and then we reach what I think are a couple of weekend places. The surveyor described them both as being 'in a poor condition'. 'Doris Lodge' is the first one we come to. It's a timber building with an asbestos tile roof and only one room. Asbestos tiles seem quite popular round here! Next to it is a timber hut that doesn't even have a name.

We are now reaching the crossroads with Devonshire Road. This is the end of the unmade section of King Edward Road. On the right-hand corner is a bungalow called 'Roselandia'. In 1949 it was described as being 'a four-roomed stucco building in a good condition with a tile roof'. It was owned by William and Winifred Kemp. When I first started riding my bike and asked to ride outside our garden my mum would say, 'Okay, but only as far as the Kemps', as she didn't like me going on to the made-up road.

The made-up section of King Edward Road stretches out in front of us and leads down to Laindon High Road. Halfway along there used be to a farm, I believe, called Whitehouse Farm, where a flock of very aggressive geese used to attack any passers-by. My brother accidently ran over one on his bike when it rushed out in front of him and he couldn't stop in time. During my childhood, the area where the farm had stood became the playfield between King Edward Road and Powell Road. I walk across it every day on my way home from school. The local children really appreciate that field and many games of football, rounders and cricket are played there. It is also the site for an enormous bonfire on Guy Fawkes Night each year. However, I hear rumours they are planning to build tower blocks on the site – I hope that's not true.

Let's head back down King Edward Road and look at the plots on the opposite side of the road. Mind the puddles as you cross. On the corner opposite 'Roselandia' is a bungalow called 'St Malo'. It's a two-roomed timber building with asbestos tile roof. Next to it is 'Jessamine', which was described in exactly the same way in the survey. It was owned by James, Emma and William Kemp, who were probably relatives of the Kemps from 'Roselandia'. There are greenhouses in the plot next door, but I'm not sure whether they belong to 'Jessamine'.

The next bungalow is called 'Tre-Pol-Pen' and it is directly opposite 'California'. It had originally been built in 1931 and named 'Clemrich'. Its first owners were Jimmy Richards (my dad's best friend from Richards'

'Clemrich' in 1931.

farm) and Maria Clements (my nan's niece). They moved into it when they married, and their daughter Hilda was born there. In 1949 it was described as 'a two-roomed stucco building with asbestos tile roof in a fair condition'. Little did the surveyors know that it had actually been built from old orange boxes! The Richards moved elsewhere and for a short while Ethel and Joseph Cook lived there.

A few years ago Don and Myrtle Jones moved in. They are a very nice Cornish couple, who keep chickens and sell eggs. I believe they changed the name of the bungalow to 'Tre-Pol-Pen'. I remember late one afternoon, we saw smoke across the Top Field coming from the direction of 'Tre-Pol-Pen'. Myself, along with my Mum, my brother, Alan, and nephew, Paul, walked across to see what was happening. As we got nearer we saw that the outbuildings were on fire. Myrtle was very distressed and my Mum tried to comfort her. The wind was blowing the flames toward the chicken shed and she was frightened for the chickens that were inside. The fire brigade had been sent for but hadn't yet arrived.

Very quickly the fire spread and indeed the chicken shed caught alight and was quickly ablaze, causing Myrtle to sob. Before we could stop him, Paul dashed to the shed, flung the door open and went inside through the smoke. He pushed the window open from inside and started throwing the startled chickens out, and didn't stop until he had rescued every one. He then emerged just as the fire brigade was arriving. Paul's quick thinking was reported in the *Laindon Recorder* – the hero of the day.

Rather than walking back along 'The Boards' round to 'Spion Kop', we will take the short cut across the Top Field. You can see a well-worn grass track diagonally across the field which will bring us out to a gate in front of 'Rosedene'. This track is very muddy at the moment, but looking at the state of our footwear I don't think we can make matters much worse. When we reach the gate we will turn right and it is only a short walk to 'Spion Kop'. Hopefully we can cadge a cup of tea from my mum while we let our feet dry out.

Back to Reality

Welcome back to the present, where we can find out what the area is like today. In the mid-'60s a new housing estate was built at Bourne Close, and a block of garages appeared alongside the garden of 'Spion Kop'. Although the appearance of new houses was

Sylvia Richards outside 'Sunnymead', 1934. 'Pendennis' in the background. The hedge now runs along the edge of Ford's site.

not ideal, it did give the teenage Nina cause to celebrate because she was then able to access Bourne Close from her garden and no longer needed to walk the unmade boards. A whole world of fashionable shoes was then opened up to her.

However, the creeping advance of new housing did herald the end of the plotland existence for Nina's family. By 1975 their plot was compulsorily purchased by Basildon Development Corporation and life at 'Spion Kop' came to an end. The acre of land is now under houses and maisonettes at the end of Bourne Avenue. Housing also covers the former unmade section of King Edward Road. Tower blocks were indeed built on the playing field along the made-up part of King Edward Road in the 1960s, but these are due for demolition soon.

Coopers' field, that Nina's dad once looked after so carefully, has been left to return to scrub as part of Victoria Park. The remains of the Coopers' bungalow, 'The Retreat', are deep inside the dense tangled undergrowth. Nina says that its well is still there, with its secret contents of bottles and tin cans hidden far below.

Alexandra Road is now part of Victoria Park. Walkers straying from the path might still find remnants of some of the former plots among the bushes. The 'Pendennis' plot is now overgrown with scrub; the site of its neighbour 'Rosedene' is open grassland.

Looking at an aerial map on the internet you can see that many of the surrounding fields, such as 'Snaggs', are now under the car park belonging to Ford's Research Centre. The site of the Richards' former farmhouse, 'Sunnymead', is in a bushy area running alongside the Ford's site. An old fence post is still visible.

However, there is one important relic from Nina's childhood that still exists on a patch of greensward between the houses which stand in 'her garden'. We discovered it when we returned to the site in autumn 2009. Nina had not visited the area since her family left in 1975 as it had been too painful to see what had become of her childhood haven. In particular, she had been told that all the trees in her garden, including her favourite oak tree, had been felled when the land was cleared. Driving onto the estate we managed to get our bearings by starting at the block of garages that had been built in Bourne Close in the mid-1960s, and we worked out the layout of the plot from there. The grey drizzle seemed to suit the mood as we surveyed the row of houses in Bourne Avenue which dissected the once sweeping lawn with its long herbaceous border. A tatty pair of old armchairs had been dumped on the road outside the maisonettes, roughly where Nina's old London tram would have sat.

Nina's husband, Colin, and I watched Nina wander around trying to pace out distances, knowing that she was seeing a different landscape in her mind's eye. Colin, a keen naturalist, was surveying the trees trying to work out whether any of them were old enough to have been in the garden over thirty years before, but he decided that most were too young. He pointed to a row of houses at what would have been the end of the garden, asking Nina whether that was where their pond would have been. She agreed, adding that the pond had been near her favourite oak tree. Colin headed across the patch of grass, and it was then that he spotted it – a fine old oak! Nina could instantly tell it was her oak by the shape of its branches, and she galloped towards it like a young child. Seeing the expression of joy on her face is something I will never forget. I will let Nina give us some final words.

> My highlight of this autumn was returning to Alexandra Road with Deanna. It was an emotional experience filled with joy and sadness. Those times are long gone but evidence still remains of the plots that once existed there. The boundaries between the plots can still be clearly seen if you know where to look, and I do. What had been Alexandra Road is now called Victoria Park.
>
> The biggest thrill was discovering that our oak tree, which I thought had long been disposed of, is still standing. I gave it a hug, wiped a tear from my eye and gathered some acorns. I took them home with me in my coat pocket.

For me, watching Nina gather those acorns was a special moment that seemed to symbolise that the plotland spirit, like nature herself, still endures.

'Spion Kop' from oak tree, 1970s.

Same view from oak tree, 2009.

Chapter 9

The High Bank Estate

Until the mid-1980s if we had crossed the railway bridge near Dunton Drive (now the westerly end of the Durham Road extension) we would have entered the plotlands that formed the High Bank Estate and Berry Park Estates. The former was where my family owned 'Halliford' in High Bank Drive, and I focused extensively on this estate in my first book, *Basildon Plotlands*. Although I will include a few photographs of the plots owned by my friends and family to give a portrait of the overall area, I won't be retelling their stories or mine.

The plots on these estates started to become available after plots on the Dunton Hills Estate had been put up for sale in the 1920s. Wandering down the grassy lanes it was impossible to tell where one estate ended and the other began, as they joined seamlessly.

There were around 266 plots in the lanes which made up these two estates at the time of the 1949 survey; 77 per cent of these were one-roomed buildings, and 99 per cent of the properties were of timber construction (of which only 10 per cent were rendered). Fifty-three per cent of the roofs were clad with felt.[1]

With a few exceptions, most lanes were predominantly used by weekenders and some were occupied solely by weekenders. This contrasts with the estate to the west of Laindon, which we considered in an earlier chapter, where the properties tended to be larger and more residents lived there permanently.

Today the combined site of the High Bank and Berry Park Estates is roughly bordered by Mandeville Way to the north, Hawthorn Path to the east (which runs from the Great Berry open space to the railway bridge), Forest Glade to the south, and Tesco and the Langdon Reserve to the west. High View Avenue runs through the middle from Mandeville Way to Forest Glade. I have seen a map from the mid-1980s which showed the plotland lanes overlaid with the proposed new roads. The new High View Avenue followed the course of its predecessor, bending slightly to bisect Hill Top Rise through the plot next to 'The Cabin' and 'Tekowaia' opposite (owned by Mrs Jeeves) and then continuing to cut a swathe through Arcadian Gardens, Highland Gardens and

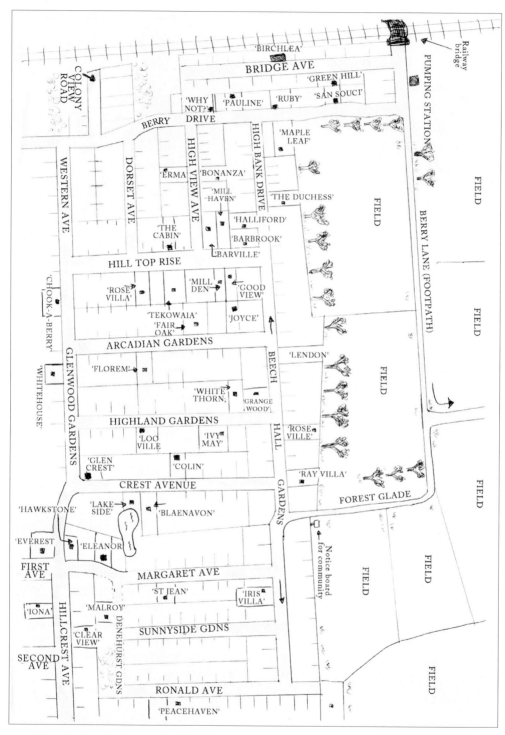

Map showing the plots on the High Bank and Berry Park Estates which feature in this book.

Crest Avenue. A former member of the Planning Office told me that the road was designed to bend round established trees which they wanted to retain.

Let us look in detail at a few of the lanes on the High Bank Estate and hear the memories of some former plotlanders who lived there. We will look at Berry Park in the next chapter.

Bridge Avenue

Bridge Avenue was the first turning on the right just after the railway bridge. It had a better surface than most, having a layer of hardcore on it. In 1949 there were 24 properties spread on either side of the lane (18 timber or plywood and six with stucco rendering). Many residents lived there permanently. Today, Bridge Avenue has disappeared under Mandeville Way, but the gardens must lurk in the undergrowth bordering the road. To me, there is still something familiar about one of the large oaks which stands at the roadside. It was probably in one of the gardens that I passed on a regular basis.

Berry Drive

Near its junction with Berry Lane (which today has been renamed Hawthorn Path where it intersects with Nottingham Way) there was a large field bordered by huge oak trees. These were shown on the map that accompanied the 1949 survey with a note from the surveyor that 'these trees should be maintained'. In the early 1970s someone undertook some savage maintenance when all the trees were cut down. This significantly altered the character of the lane. Berry Drive disappeared from the map in the 1990s when a new housing estate was built on it, and Nottingham Way now roughly follows its path.

In 1949 there were 23 timber properties listed in this lane, two of which were rendered with stucco. The Electoral Register from the same year shows that at least half the residents lived there permanently.[2]

'Ruby'

Phylis Frasi grew up in 'Ruby' in Berry Drive but also lived in Bridge Avenue. Her family owned a number of plots in the area, at least four plots in Berry Drive alone. Her uncle bought one at the end near Berry Lane, her parents owned 'Ruby', her grandmother Mrs Humberstone owned 'Pauline' and at some point another of her uncles lived in 'Sunningdale'. She also had relatives living on the other side of the railway in 'Algar' in Worthing Avenue.

Her parents moved from Holloway Road in London around 1939 and her mother lived there until the early 1980s. Their plot was described in the 1949 survey as being a two-roomed timber building in a fair condition with a corrugated iron roof. Phylis said the building was later rendered with pebble-dash. They had gas mantles for lighting and a coal fire. Water came from a well that they shared with their neighbours in 'Laureldene'.

> As a child I went to Dunton School and spent free time playing with the other plotland children, so I knew many people who lived in the nearby lanes. We really used to enjoy playing around the railway bridge and in a ditch that ran alongside a field opposite, where people would dump their rubbish.

Phylis in the garden of 'Ruby' in the 1950s. 'Laureldene' can be seen next door.

I remember Phylis's widowed mother living there alone in the 1970s as my mum would sometimes stop to chat with her at the gate. 'Ruby' was opposite Ern South's plot 'Maple Leaf', and in *Basildon Plotlands* I mentioned that Ern always called his neighbour 'A.D.A.' I didn't know why, but Phylis has cleared up the mystery by explaining that Ada was her mum's middle name.

Phylis married in 1962 and went to live in 'Green Hill' in Bridge Avenue for a few months. She then moved into a caravan (which they named 'Cherry') on Thomas West's plot 'Birchlea' in Bridge Avenue and lived there for 18 months in 1962-3. A lot of the plots were still occupied then. While she was living there she remembers a sad incident:

> One day the elderly couple who lived next door were found gassed in their hut. We knew there was something wrong when my husband heard their dog whimpering at the door, so we got the police. They forced the door and found the couple.

Roughly opposite Mr West's property was a plot owned by the Rentcombe family, who had a timber shack and a couple of caravans. Their land backed onto the Frasi's bungalow in Berry Drive behind. I can remember there being a narrow overgrown path next to them which linked the two lanes in the 1970s.

Their neighbours were the Paynes who lived in 'The Roost', and Phylis remembers getting supplies of paraffin from them. She added, 'One year their son dug a huge hole in their garden and buried an old car in it.' I wonder whether that was ever discovered when Mandeville Way was built.

It seems that Mrs Payne sold the plot to her niece Maud Sargent after the war. She soon realised that she had taken on more than expected. Maud explained that when her aunt moved, 'the weekenders had nowhere to buy paraffin and as we had all the equipment we decided to … [sell] it or else they had to walk to Lower Dunton Road'.[3]

There were only a couple of permanent residents who were still living in Bridge Avenue by the late 1970s: Mr West and his dog, Peter, and the Boniface Family of 'Tall Trees'.

Phylis's mother decided to move from 'Ruby' in the early 1980s as the character of the plotlands was changing. Building work just over the bridge had brought the town too close. Phylis explains how difficult things became for her mum:

> The final straw came when she arrived home one day
> to find her bungalow had been ransacked. The police
> didn't seem very interested as so many break-ins were
> happening at the time, but I had a right go at them and
> got them round.

'Ruby' was compulsorily purchased by the Corporation shortly afterwards and Mrs Frasi moved to Langdon Hills. She didn't receive very much money for the plot as she was told that the land would be reverting to agricultural use. A housing estate was built there in the 1990s.

Phylis kept in touch with several of the elderly plotlanders after they had to leave their homes. She regularly visited Mr West when he moved into sheltered accommodation, and with her husband and a dumper truck she helped Mrs Jeeves to move from 'Tekowaia' in Hill Top Rise into sheltered accommodation in the 1980s.

'Maple Leaf'

'Maple Leaf' in Berry Drive was originally owned by the Seeley family from the 1930s to the 1950s. It gained its name because Mr Seeley came from Canada and remained in England when he

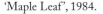
'Maple Leaf', 1984.

married. In 1949 it was described as a one-roomed timber building in a poor condition with a felt roof. At some point the plot was bought by Ernest South, who lived there until 1984. I remember Ern very well, and we used to have many chats with him. Below, Mark McManus gives an account of meeting Ern just before he moved out:

'Maple Leaf' was the last bungalow to exist in Berry Drive. By the time I came to know it, the sole occupants were an elderly gentleman named Ernest South and a very excitable black puppy called Bob [his previous dog called Bob had recently died].

I spoke to Ern on three occasions, although his accent – and habit of talking in a growl – made him occasionally difficult to understand! The first time I hailed him, as he was pottering in his garden, he was rather gruff and uncommunicative, although the puppy made up for it with exuberant friendliness. I suspected that his attitude stemmed from the fact that the large and sprawling housing estate just over the railway line, constructed a few years before, had caused an influx of youths on motorbikes to the tracks of the plotland area – and 'Maple Leaf', now devoid of neighbours for a considerable distance, was vulnerable as the first building these unwelcome visitors would come across.

The second time I met with Ern, he was a little friendlier – possibly because I handed over a bag of apples as a gift. On that occasion, he opened the front gate of his plot and allowed Bob to scamper around my feet, seemingly pleased with the considerable fuss I made of his companion. It was fortuitous that I was always a dog lover.

The final time I met Ern, he seemed a little restless, although he was reticent to explain why. A few weeks later, I passed 'Maple Leaf', glanced over the front gate and my heart sank. The windows of the bungalow stared back at me, vacant and sightless, denuded of their net curtains. 'Maple Leaf' was empty.

I remember the regret I felt as I opened the gate and trudged towards the building. In the few months I had known the Dunton plotlands, I had already seen some of its few surviving buildings disappear ... this was the first time I had experienced the loss of a full-time resident, although, sadly, it was not to be the last.

The back door was unlocked and I quietly slipped in, for my first and last visit to the interior of 'Maple Leaf'. All furniture was gone, but the presence of Ern

South and his puppy still lingered in the aroma of the place, the unmistakable scent of dog and old clothing. On the floor of the front room I found a train ticket. It told me of a journey undertaken from London to Laindon, but a week previously. Wherever Ern and Bob had disappeared to, I silently wished them luck.

Nick Street, who worked for the Corporation's Planning and Transportation Department, remembers helping Ern to move. Ern was desperate to be rehoused because he was suffering from harassment from gangs of youths, and life had become unbearable. Nick said they were able to find Ern a suitable new home and move him within a week of receiving his plea for help.

High Bank Drive

This was the lane where my family's plot, 'Halliford', was located, and my parents owned it from 1954-83. I only remember two dwellings being used regularly by the 1980s – our plot and the neighbouring 'Barbrook' owned by Nell King. However, in 1949 this lane comprised 14 plots, all of which were one-roomed timber shacks, primarily used by weekenders. There were also a couple of large plots described as wasteland. Our plot was described as 'derelict' in the survey, and 'Barbrook' described as being timber with a felt roof. However, the Kings made improvements, rendering it with pebbledash and adding a curved corrugated iron roof.

Hill Top Rise

The 1949 survey listed 16 one-roomed buildings in this lane, with several other plots described as being wasteland. Fifteen were made from timber, of which 13 had felt roofs, one had a corrugated iron roof and one had asbestos tiles. One building was constructed from asbestos sheets and had a corrugated iron roof – classy!

Below: Glad Darwin and niece Sylvia outside the rear of 'Halliford', mid-1960s. 'Colyea' can be seen opposite in High Bank Drive.

Below right: The front garden of 'Barbrook', mid-1960s.

The Nyes playing golf at 'Mill Haven'. 'Good View' and 'Mill Den' in background.

Glad at side entrance to 'Mill Haven', mid-1960s.

'The Cabin' in the late 1970s. Left to right: Nell from 'Barbrook', Jil, Jean and Ray Dickinson.

The Nyes at 'Barville', mid-1960s.

My mum's brother Con owned 'Mill Haven' from the early 1950s until it fell out of use in the late 1960s. In the 1949 survey it was already named 'Mill Haven' and was described as being a 'one-roomed, timber building with felt roof in a poor condition'. The overall plot was judged to be 'untidy'.

Opposite were two plots that were still in use in the 1970s: 'Good View', which was used very occasionally by weekenders from Dagenham, and 'Mill Den', which was lived in permanently by a couple named Glad and Alf Langford. They moved out around 1977.

By the 1980s there were several weekend properties still in regular use: 'The Cabin', owned by the Dickinsons since 1962; 'Barville', owned by the Nyes; and 'Rose Villa', owned by the Striplings. Mrs Jeeves of 'Tekowaia' was the lane's last permanent resident and when her plot was compulsorily purchased she moved into sheltered accommodation in Laindon.

'Rose Villa'

Gladys Fenn explains below how her family owned 'Rose Villa' from the early 1930s until the mid-1980s.

Alf Stripling enjoying the peace of 'Rose Villa'.

My great grandfather Benjamin Stripling was a coal merchant and also a bit of a speculator. He used to buy up plots of land from all over and just kept them for investment purpose. With this in mind, he encouraged his son Alfred Stripling – my grandfather – to do the same. So in the early 1930s Alf purchased a plot of ground in Hill Top Rise. It was bought as a present for his wife Bertha so it was registered in her name. It lay empty for several years.

Alfred's daughter Florence, 'Auntie Florrie', first remembers going to Laindon when she was 12-13 years old around 1936. There was no hut or building of any kind, just a plot of ground. The first time they went the family who owned the plot next to them already had a hut, so invited them in for a drink. There was no-where to get water and even though there was a water tap at the top of the lane at the High Bank Drive end, you had to have a key to access it. On

Gladys Stripling looking out at Hill Top Rise, 1950s.

following visits Auntie Florrie remembers taking lemonade with them.

To obtain a key to the water tap, you needed to have a dwelling place on the land. So my grandfather ordered an empty wooden crate to be delivered by truck to the site and converted it into a hut.

Following the outbreak of the Second World War, once London was suffering from bomb attacks, my grandfather decided the plot at Laindon would be a safe place to evacuate his wife and children to whilst he stayed behind in London to run the coal business. Any furniture they could spare from their home in Leytonstone was taken to Laindon on the coal cart. When it reached the top of Berry Lane, the track was not suitable for the horse and cart – so all the furniture had to be carried from there to Hill Top Rise.

At weekends my grandfather would join his family at Laindon and set to work building a proper hut to join onto the front of the container. This part was raised on proper blocks and had a central door with a push-out window on either side. This half became the bedroom.

My own mother, Gladys, who was born in 1931, had told me of an incident when she was about eight years old. Whilst walking down one of the lanes, a bomb was dropped in the area and they had to jump into a ditch and crouch there in the dark until they thought it was safe to move. I believe after that incident my grandfather told my uncle that he had to move down with them and he would have had to make the journey back to London daily by train to go to work.

As the family were now living more permanently at Hill Top Rise, they had to give a name to the property for postal purposes. They were not the kind of people to

spend time thinking of a fancy name so my grandmother
just settled on the name of 'Rose Villa', simply
because the group of terraced houses at their home in
Leytonstone were called Rose Villas.

Following their engagement party at Laindon,
Florence Stripling married Walter Biggs in March 1952.
As there was a housing shortage in London, they lived
at Laindon for the first summer of their marriage. By the
time the autumn came and the nights were drawing in,
they decided to find a flat back in Leytonstone. It was
now November so it must have been pretty cold in the
wooden hut with no heating, just a Calor Gas stove for
cooking and heating water.

In 1954 Gladys Stripling married Eric Biggs, twin
brother of Walter Biggs. Eric Biggs worked for Barnett
Ensign, who made the Brownie Box cameras. As my dad,
Eric, was interested in photography, the family have him
to thank for the photographic memories that he took in
the 1950s, which he developed himself.

The first visit every spring, the grass would be a foot
high and the men would cut it with scythes. All the hay
would then be stacked outside the plot in the lane like
a haystack and all the children would jump in it. The
ladies would sit outside with grandma shelling garden
peas for lunch. A wheelbarrow was made from a wooden

The Biggs
blackberrying
in Hill Top Rise
near junction with
Western Avenue,
late 1970s.

'Rose Villa' in late
1970s, with Gladys,
Tina and Eric Biggs.

Exercise at 'Bonanza', High View Avenue, in the days before Wii-fit. 'Lydmouth' can be seen next door. Mid-1960s.

greengrocer's box with old pram wheels attached, and two milk churns were placed inside to collect the water in.

Once the grandchildren started to arrive there were to be many lazy days spent in the countryside in the 1960s and 1970s, walking around the gradually overgrowing lanes, picking blackberries and scrumping for apples on abandoned plots.

In 1984 Mark McManus walked around the area and noted that:

> The only shack remaining in Hill Top Rise was called 'Rose Villa', and that collapsed – or more likely was pushed over – a few weeks later. However, the wooden floor lasted for another 18 months or so, hidden by grass.

In chapter 16 Mark McManus continues with a moving account of discovering the last remaining plots in this area in 1984.

High View Avenue
There were 11 properties listed in the 1949 survey, all of which were one-roomed timber buildings. Ten had a felt roof and one ('Redriff') had gone upmarket and used slates. The surveyor described most of the plots as being used by weekenders, and I cannot recall mention of any permanent residents living there.

Next we will look at the Berry Park Estate.

Chapter 10

The Berry Park Estate

Walking from the High Bank Estate to the Berry Park Estate brought no major changes in the plotland landscape. The once well-trimmed hawthorn and blackthorn hedges had grown into sprawling bushes, and white poplars and brambles fought fierce battles to colonise former plots.

Beech Hall Gardens
I remember Beech Hall Gardens as a very long grassy track with a narrow concrete path which ran from the water tap at the junction with Hill Top Rise down to the junction with Forest Glade and beyond, finishing at the junction with Ronald Avenue. A line of towering elms provided an impressive backdrop to the plots on the eastern side, and separated the gardens from the meadow behind. During the 1970s these magnificent trees were reduced to skeletal remains as Dutch elm disease ravaged the countryside.

Today, part of the meadow still exists as open space. In the autumn of 2009 I walked along the path that skirts round the edge of the playing field running parallel with the new Forest Glade, and then turns right towards the new housing. I realised that the footpath was roughly following the track of its predecessor along Beech Hall Gardens. Walking along that path I felt very frustrated when I reached the houses in Oakham Close and Lancaster Drive because my fantasy of magically being transported back to the 1970s was shattered. The site of our plot in High Bank Drive was probably not much more than a hundred yards further on, but only a landscape of bricks, concrete and parked cars confronted me.

In the 1949 survey there were 38 properties listed in Beech Hall Gardens. Twenty-four were one-roomed, and 14 were estimated to be two-roomed. Thirty-three were described as being timber or wood, four had been rendered with stucco and one was brick. The condition of the plots was typically mixed, with 22 judged to be kept/tidy/well kept and 13 untidy or badly kept. As it was such a long lane, it was actually surveyed by two surveyors, which is why there are different ways of describing the condition of the plots.[1]

Let's take a look at a couple of the plots in this lane.

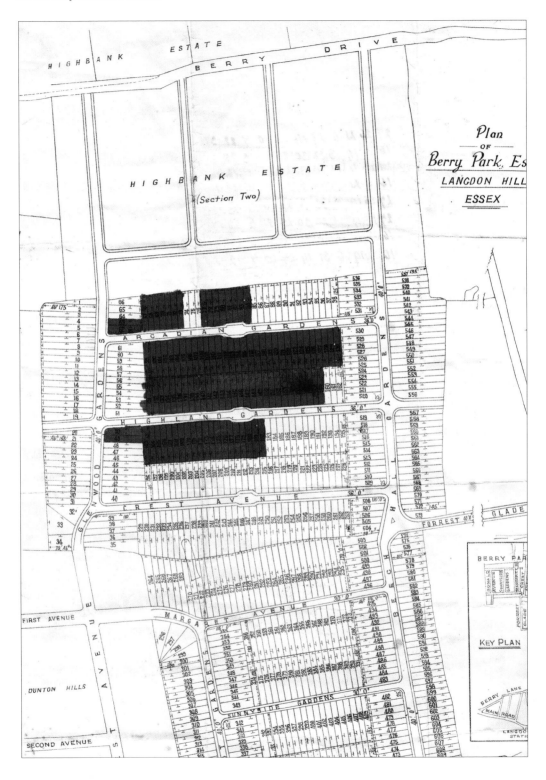

Opposite: Sales
particulars from mid-
1920s when plots on
the Berry Park Estate
were being sold.

'Lendon'

Joan Tivendale's maternal grandparents, Annie and Sam Roberts, bought this plot in 1937/8 after spotting an advert in one of the London local newspapers. The family travelled from Bow to spend weekends there until they sold it to a Mr Walker in 1954.

The plot was named after its builders, Len and Don. In 1949 it was described as being a one-roomed stucco building with an asbestos tiled roof. Joan's mother, Phyl, remembers it having two rooms, a bedroom and a living room. Lighting came from oil lamps, and heating from paraffin heaters and a range in the living room. A shed in the garden was used for cooking by paraffin cooker, and for doing washing using rainwater collected in a barrel. The family had an affectionate name for the toilet at the end of the garden – 'The Thunderbox'.

The family paid 6d. a week for the upkeep of the path along Beech Hall Gardens which led round to Forest Glade. They also paid to use the water tap near Hill Top Rise.

Until her parents bought a car in 1953, the family travelled by train and either walked from the station or paid a man with a

Annie Roberts at 'Lendon'.

Beech Hall Gardens. 'Grangewood' on left is at the junction with Highland Gardens. 1984.

Annie, Phyl and Joan at 'Lendon', early 1950s.

private car half a crown to drive them the rest of the way. As with most families the plot became the focus for family gatherings with aunts, uncles and extended family visiting regularly. A tent was erected on busy weekends and Joan remembers it was a real treat to be allowed to sleep in it.

Their plot backed onto a field where cows grazed. From my estimations I think the site of their plot is currently in a stretch of undeveloped land which runs alongside the open space roughly opposite the end of Northampton Grove.

'Iris Villa'

Dave Anderson's grandparents owned 'Iris Villa', which stood in the section of Beech Hall Gardens just beyond Forest Glade and Margaret Avenue. I have had the pleasure of meeting Dave and his wife, Jean, on several occasions since Dave first contacted me after *Basildon Plotlands* was published. He loved his trips to stay at 'Iris Villa' as a young boy and his memories of roaming the countryside have always been very special to him. Dave and I both agree that there is something magical about spending your childhood in the plotlands, and some of that magic never leaves you.

Around 1937 his grandparents, Henry and Mary Anderson, bought the plot of land, which was approximately 150 feet wide and 200 feet long. They moved there permanently from Hackney after Henry retired from the Hackney police. He must have been a reassuring presence in the plotlands as he had earned a commendation from Lord Trenchard in 1922 for 'vigilance and promptitude in capturing burglars'.

Named after their daughter, Iris, the plot was described in the 1949 survey as a two-roomed wooden building with an asbestos tiled roof and a greenhouse. Overall the plot was judged to be well kept, which will be good news to Dave. After all, no one wants to discover that their treasured family plot has been described as an untidy hovel.

Henry and Mary Anderson outside 'Iris Villa', mid-1940s.

The survey underestimated the size of the building, as can be seen from Dave's description:

> At the front of the bungalow there was a rockery and a wooden arch that you had to go through coming in the front gate. We normally entered the bungalow at the back door that led directly into the pantry that had a larder at one end. This room ran from front to back on the left-hand side as you look at the front of the bungalow. The living room was where all the

Dave's mother, Rose Anderson, in garden of 'Iris Villa'. 'Acacia' or 'Essex Villa' in background. 1950s.

cooking took place on a range. There were two bedrooms, one had a single bed and the other had a double. In the large bedroom was a large chest of draws and we always seemed to have apples wrapped up in newspaper in it. This always gave that bedroom a lovely smell.

In common with other residents of the estate, the Andersons used Tilley lamps and candles to light the bungalow, and collected water in buckets from the water tap at the end of Forest Glade.

When Henry passed away in 1946, Mary continued to live there on her own for a year. Unfortunately she broke her leg and found it too difficult to manage on her own, so moved back to Hackney to live with her son. The bungalow then became a weekend retreat for the family until they sold it to Basildon Development Corporation in 1962.

Dave remembers family and friends gathering at the plot for fun once the labour-intensive chore of mowing the lawn was completed:

> We would play cricket and golf in the back garden. Uncle Len had cut six holes in the lawn and we had our own little golf course. At night it was great. We would be sat around the table in the living room, only lit by a single Tilley lamp which made such a wonderful hissing noise – it was almost a hypnotic sound. If we were lucky we would have the radio on if the batteries had not run out. They didn't last very long in those days.

107

Dave (taking a rest from roaming) and his nan in garden of 'Iris Villa'.

I went to bed with a candle, in a candle-stick holder of course, and would read my favourite book 'Rupert the Bear'. When I woke up in the morning I would see the sun shining through the curtains and hear the cockerel from the garden of the bungalow opposite.

As a child he spent a lot of time roaming around the lanes on foot or later on his bike. He would often earn pocket money picking mushrooms in a field nearby and sometimes went to play along Hillcrest Avenue. 'Kite flying was great at the top of any of the avenues as there was nearly always a stiff breeze.'

Dave recalls that as he spent a lot of time outside, his mother would rub him with vinegar to prevent sunburn. He said that he constantly smelled like a bag of chips. Perhaps some ex-plotlanders might remember always becoming overwhelmed with the urge to visit a fish shop whenever a certain young boy wandered past their plot.

Highland Gardens

This was one of the grassy lanes leading off Beech Hall Gardens. Original site plans show it being 36 feet wide with single plots having a frontage of 20 feet and a depth of 115 feet. These were pretty common dimensions, though most people would buy several plots. In 1949 there were 15 properties in the lane, of which eight were described as being timber, six stucco and one made from asbestos sheets. With one exception they were all judged to be one- or two-roomed buildings. 'Grangewood', owned by the Haybells, stood at the corner of the lane.

'Looville'

This plot was owned by Jean Darby in the late 1940s and 1950s. The survey noted that it was a stucco building with an asbestos tile roof and was in a very untidy condition. With an estimated four rooms this was one of the largest properties on the estate. Jean said that in fact it had six rooms.

Jean's family originated from East Ham and before the war her father bought five plots of land

in Dorset Avenue, on which they erected a shed and a tent and which they used for weekends. When war broke out they moved down permanently and bought four plots of land in Highland Gardens on which 'Looville' stood. With such a large plot they had plenty of fruit trees and kept chickens and rabbits. Her husband's family lived in the next lane, Western Avenue.

She recalls how difficult it was to manage there once she had her three babies:

> In the winter it was really hard not having water and proper heating. We only had paraffin lamps and later got a Calor Gas stove. Often the local standpipe was frozen and Mr Ray from 'Ray Villa' in Beech Hall Gardens would try to thaw it out by lighting a small fire under it. I had to break ice from our water tanks just to wash the nappies. When I was pregnant I had to walk all the way to Berry Lane on the unmade paths in winter just to meet the ambulance as it couldn't get any closer.

She tried for many years to get a Corporation house but she wasn't in a priority group. At the time the Corporation was still trying to ensure that it could house key workers who were needed to make the New Town flourish, meet its responsibilities to the London Boroughs and rehouse those whose plots it had demolished for new development. Jean was not in one of these groups. She put her name down on the local council's waiting list, but it was not easy to get council housing as the council was restricted in the number of houses it could build due to the constraints of Basildon's Master Plan. She explained that the prioritisation of people from outside Basildon for housing did cause resentment among the locals at the time.

'Ivy May'

This very large plot was four down from 'Looville' and was owned by William and Philadelphia Stace in the 1930s and 1940s. Their grandson Ron Powell remembers staying with them when he was a boy. According to the Electoral Register they were still living there in 1949. The survey described the property as a two-roomed timber building in a fair condition with an asbestos tile roof. Today the site of 'Ivy May' is roughly under High View Avenue.

Ron's grandparents originated from Manor Park but moved to live permanently in 'Ivy May'. He used to visit for weekends in the 1930s, but during the war he went to live with them while his father was away in the navy and his mother remained with his siblings in Dagenham. In the latter part of the war his mother rented and later bought a bungalow called 'Lil Villa' in New Avenue, which was the road leading to the Recreation Ground just off Berry Lane. Ron recalls what it was like living in 'Ivy May':

Uncle Bill Stace in garden of 'Ivy May', 1940s.

It was hard going, but it was still wonderful down there. Naturally we had no electricity or water. My grandfather attached wheels to a galvanised water tank and we would wheel it down to the tap at the corner of Beech Hall Gardens and Forest Glade.

We had 'posh' oil lamps that were fixed to the wall on arms. Aluminium bowls, shaped like Chinese hats, were screwed to the ceiling. They used to catch the soot and stop the ceiling going black. It was my job to clean them every week.

The plot of land was huge. We grew loads of vegetables, had fruit trees and kept chickens. There was a large outhouse where my grandmother would do the washing using a boiler heated with wood. I remember she also used the outhouse to hang muslin bags full of soft fruit to make jellies. We'd go round collecting blackberries and other fruit, and she'd squeeze the juice through the muslins.

My grandfather usually had a pony and trap which he kept on the land. He was skilled with his hands and he used to repair traps and sell them on. I can remember watching him carefully attaching spokes to the cart wheels. One day, and this is the honest truth, he asked me and my brother if we wanted to go for a ride with him. Off we set in the pony and trap and went all the way to Wickford. When we got there we watched him shaking hands with a man. He'd sold the pony and trap and we had to walk all the way home! It was a stinking hot day and when we reached *The Fortune of War* pub he went in for a drink, leaving us sitting outside. He bought us each a packet of crisps to keep us going, and my brother had to go and ask for something for us to drink! Finally we were rewarded with a lemonade.

I had to go to school at Langdon Hills and later Laindon High School. It was a really long walk along all those unmade roads, but you got used to it. On Sundays I would walk to a shop

One of William's horses in the garden of 'Ivy May', 1940s.

in Laindon High Road and buy a load of newspapers off them. Then I'd go round the plotlands selling them to the locals, adding a ha'penny on for the service. The long walk didn't bother me, and neither did the dogs. If they snarled at me as I walked to the doors I would just be firm with them, so they never went for me. I had about 20-30 customers and I saved all my money to put towards a bike. I was very proud when I eventually managed to buy one.

Like my parents, my aunts, uncles and cousins used to pop down to 'Ivy May' regularly. Often my grandparents would ask some of the other plot owners down Highlands Gardens if they would rent out their plots for a weekend or week if they weren't using them. My relations would then put up tents in the gardens to give them more room if they were only renting a one-bedroomed place.

'White Thorn'

This weekend plot was on the opposite side of the lane to 'Ivy May' near the corner with Beech Hall Gardens. It was owned by Marian Berry's grandparents who lived in Whitethorn Road in Bow, hence the name of their plot. They bought the land in the 1920s, so would have been one of the first families on the estate.

Marian has lovely memories of staying in the wilds of the countryside and she still draws strength from them now. However, she does recall that there were downsides. In particular she remembers how fumes from paraffin lamps and from their neighbour's generator were not good for her mother's health. Once her mother had a severe asthma attack in the middle of the night and had to take herself off to the doctor in Laindon. With no phone or means of transport this was her only option, and it was a frightening incident for all concerned.

Crest Avenue

This was another of the grassy lanes leading off Beech Hall Gardens. It contained 17 properties in 1949, 12 of which were described in the survey as being wooden huts, and the rest described as simply wood. Nearly all were thought to be weekend properties, and it seems that the plots were generally not in a good condition, 11 being described as either 'unkept', 'waste', 'badly kept' or 'partly kept'.

'Blaenavon'

Karen Garner's family owned 'Blaenavon'. In 1949 it was described as a one-roomed wooden building in a fair condition with an asbestos tile roof. However, in contrast to most of its neighbours, the plot was at least described as 'kept'. Karen recalls her visits:

> I can remember pushing the car up First Avenue to get to our chalet – the roads were just dirt tracks so if it had

rained the tracks were very muddy and many a time the car got stuck in a rut. If Dad had loaded the car a lot we had to walk up the hill and meet him at the top.

We had to get water in containers from the end of the road – we tended to go mostly to the Beech Hall Gardens end or if it was a nice day we'd drag our wheelbarrow containing glass dairy bottles, a small milk churn and 2-3 tin containers back to First Avenue where the water pipe was on the corner of the 'Hawkestone' chalet.

At the beginning of the season Dad would dig a big hole, and each weekend he'd empty the Elsan down the hole and just cover it with a light covering of earth. I never wanted to use the toilet after dark because of the spiders which would hang off the ceiling on long webs – horrible. So we had a potty that dad would empty into the Elsan in the morning.

Many plotlanders shared Karen's fear of the spiders in the outside loo. To be fair, I'm sure if we had interviewed plotland spiders for this book they would have said: 'It was lovely to be in the countryside where we could scurry freely, but we weren't too fond of those outside loos – too many two-legged plotlanders in them.'

Below, Karen mentions another common pastime – exploring derelict plots. I, too, remember spending many afternoons wandering around musty, dark, tumbledown buildings or fighting through hawthorn scrub and chest-high grass to pick cooking apples from long-abandoned fruit trees. You had to be vigilant because the once neatly rolled lawns had been transformed by rabbits and ant-hills into hidden traps capable of twisting the ankles of those who dared to enter the overgrown gardens.

My sister, Sara, and I would go blackberrying and exploring. When the chalets were being sold to the council they would be left empty and it was exciting and scary to go into these places to see how the other half lived. Some were really good and some you wouldn't want to live in.

When I think of the freedom us children had – can you imagine going blackberry picking now with no one around? But as we got older we got fed up with going most weekends as we wanted to be with our school friends. It is only now I can appreciate what Mum and Dad were trying to give us. I would love to relive those days and show other children what it was like to have simply the peace, wildlife and time to talk and play with your parents and siblings.

'Lakeside'

Karen has memories of the plot next door, 'Lakeside':

> It was owned by a man they called Snowie who erected a very large shed which he lived in. He was something to do with the Hackney Speedway riders and many a weekend they would all come up. They'd erect an enormous army tent and a barbecue and they'd be eating until the small hours of the night – us included.

Exploring – the ruins of first shack built at 'Anthelen' in Fourth Avenue, 1984.

The most distinguishing feature of this plot was a large pond which stretched from the middle of the garden through into two plots in Margaret Avenue in the lane behind. I have been told that the pond can be seen on maps from the 19th century. Indeed it is still a feature of the area today, and helps as a landmark for anyone wishing to work out where the old plots used to be.

Peter Jackson has clear memories of exploring the pond when he was young. He used to approach from the Margaret Avenue side:

> After the bungalow in Margaret Avenue was sold and demolished, I spent a lot of time catching newts and studying the various creatures that lived in the largish pond in its garden. The newts were common and great crested newts. I was shocked one day when what I thought was a small newt in my net turned out to be a large dytiscus beetle larva, one of the most violently carnivorous occupants of the pond. The pond never dried up, even in the summer although the water level became very low. It was quite deep too, in the middle – well over my wellingtons. The occupants of the property in Crest Avenue which was opposite the pond had tried to fill it in by creating a narrow earth bank across the middle and extending the other side to drain off the water, but they never succeeded.

The pond can still be found at the end of Meadow View and close to one of the rear entrances to the Langdon Reserve. Today, the remains of a concrete path and fence posts at the former junction of Crest Avenue and Glenwood Gardens can still be seen (see p.196). They were discovered on a footpath which runs along the top of the Langdon Reserve overlooking the Dunton Balancing Lake,

which was built in the early 1990s to take the run-off from the new housing estate. There is something very atmospheric about these fence posts. Their line may now be halted by the presence of a new house, but they give the impression that they continue to exist in a different reality.

Pond situated between Crest Avenue and Margaret Avenue, 2010.

Margaret Avenue

This lane connected Beech Hall Gardens with Hillcrest Avenue and was often used as one of the routes taken by plotlanders walking from the Dunton Hills Estate to the railway station. Today, the very top end of Margaret Avenue is part of the nature reserve and has not been developed.

In 1949 the survey listed approximately 14 plots along the lane. One was of brick construction and the rest wood. The majority had tiled roofs and 10 plots were in a 'kept' or 'well kept' condition.

'Eleanor'

This plot, named after her mother, was owned by Marion Allwood's family, the Muchmores, from 1935 to 1955. Her father worked in The Criterion restaurant in Piccadilly, and then for the Port of London. He continued to travel by train from Laindon, but in his spare time built his Dunton home with the help of his brother. The asbestos and wood bungalow was built from a kit and some photos relating to its construction are shown in chapter 1. Although facilities were basic, he did manage to make a form of central heating. There were no mains services and Marion can remember water being collected from a tap at the top of Second Avenue, with her father using buckets attached to a yoke around his neck.

The plot had a large garden and orchard and was surrounded by empty plots. The pond from Crest Avenue, which was part of the 'Lakeside' plot, extended into one of the neighbouring plots in Margaret Avenue, and since this pond still exists today it is possible to work out roughly where 'Eleanor' would have stood.

Marion remembers the neighbouring lanes of Denehurst Gardens, Sunnyside Gardens and Ronald Avenue being used mainly by weekenders. The survey data backs this up as the majority of plots in these lanes were unkept or badly kept in 1949, and the surveyor had noted that they were weekend properties.

Mr Theobald was one of the few permanent residents in Sunnyside Gardens. He kept a horse in his garden and Marion recalls that during the day he would tether it in a nearby field: 'I had to be ready with a bucket and shovel and get round the field collecting the manure before one of our neighbours, Mr Lawson from 'Malroy', got there first. We certainly had some beautiful flowers and vegetables!'

Marion Allwood at 'Eleanor'. She slept in the tent in the summer. Plot in Crest Avenue behind.

Marion's siblings and cousins outside 'Eleanor'. The neighbouring Holmquest's plot in background, *c*.1939.

Eventually her mother decided that she wanted to move to a place with better facilities, so the family relocated to Archer Road in Laindon in 1955.

Ronald Avenue

This lane was at the very end of Beech Hall Gardens and bordered a vast expanse of fields. The 1949 survey showed it contained 16 one-roomed wooden huts with felt roofs which were all judged to be weekend properties, and one four-roomed wooden building with an asbestos tiled roof.

Outside 'Peacehaven' in Ronald Avenue, 1947.

'Peacehaven', as this large building was named, must have looked like a mansion in comparison with its neighbours, the majority of which were in an unkept or badly kept condition. Ken Page, the son of its owner, now lives in Australia. A number of ex-plotlanders emigrated to Australia, perhaps hoping to find new opportunities for 'frontier living'.

Ken recalls roaming around the neighbourhood with his brother and friends. He remembers one set of neighbours in particular:

> John and Sheila who lived in 'Hill Top' next to 'Vera-Joan' in Hillcrest Avenue had a bull from a very young age and the idea was to let it grow for a few months then knock it off for the meat value. It got pretty big and they tied it to a large steel spike driven into the ground on the area behind their house. The bull [possibly called Ferdie] was on a chain about 25 feet long and it used to roam in circles round the spike. As kids we used to see how close we could get to him without him getting at us. He got so big that in the end John had him carted off.

Page family at rear of 'Peacehaven', 1950s.

Peter Jackson also remembers these neighbours rearing rabbits and chickens as they were attempting to start a smallholding. He told me, 'they had a rooster which terrified me and used to chase me out of their garden when I was a small boy.'

Having heard many memories of pleasant summer days, we now want to see what winter was like in the plotlands.

Chapter 11

The Plotlands in Winter

Friday 23 April 1976
Weather on the change. Showery, cold wind and even
snow. So decided to pack up and come home.

This diary entry was written by my mum during one of the
holidays at our weekend hut. These words would probably have
been echoed throughout plots all over the Basildon countryside
as 'soft' weekenders like us decided to head back to London
at the first hint of Jack Frost's nipping frenzy. Admittedly, most
weekend properties were ill-equipped for cold weather as they
were designed for summer use. Few weekenders had open fires or
stoves suitable for heating and cooking, which were essential for
permanent residents. So what was winter like for the permanent
residents? Let's take a brief look.

One of the most challenging aspects of a cold winter was getting
a regular water supply. Those who relied on standpipes would find
them frozen solid and they had to light fires underneath them to try
to thaw them out. Similarly the rainwater in tanks could become
frozen. Nina Humphrey from 'Spion Kop' recalls her father putting
hot pokers into their tanks to break the ice.

Getting around was also a difficult business. The muddy roads
would often be impassable which is why plotlanders clubbed together
to pay for paths to be laid. Peter remembers how, ironically, icy
weather could make it easier to negotiate the lanes because the mud
had frozen solid. Snow would naturally bring its own challenges, but
the local residents often took it upon themselves to clear the paths.
David Blaine from 'Westholme' in Sidney Road remembers:

> We used to have very cold winters with snow about a
> foot deep. You had to clear the pathway and it would
> take around an hour or so. There was no such thing as
> winter grit so we would put the ashes from the fire on
> the path.

Sometimes putting ash on the path was simply inadequate.
Rod Cole was a delivery boy in the early 1960s for the Dry Street

Mrs Galpin of
'Tetherdown' walking
through 'The
Spinney' at the end
of Helmore Crescent,
1969.

Post Office stores, but his route took him around plotland lanes in Langdon Hills. He particularly remembers the harsh winter of 1962/3 when the snow had drifted so high that it was impossible to tell where the road ended and the top of a hedge began!

The log book for the plotlanders' local school on Lower Dunton Road vividly shows the difficulties the bad weather caused in February 1932:

> Snow is falling and a rough wind is driving it into the school. Attendance has fallen very low … a total of 66/112. It is exceedingly difficult to keep the room warm today, as in spite of the springs on the doors the wind forces them open. The furnace is working at its highest level.

The Head noted that it was still difficult to keep the temperature as high as 50 degrees Fahrenheit, and it was sometimes only 40 degrees.

Plotlanders' preparations for winter actually had to start in the summer. The state of the roads meant it was impossible to get coal deliveries once bad weather set in, so coal had to be bought well in advance. An invoice for Mr Davison from 'Wideview' in Helmore Crescent showed that

Helen Anthony by the range in the kitchen of 'Anthelen' on Fourth Avenue. 1950s.

Rear of Coombe Cottage, 1947.

Looking up Second Avenue, 1940s.

he had a ton of coal delivered in early September 1935 from J & R Billings of Laindon, and paid £1 1s. 0d. for his load. Jean Dallinger from Merrylands Road nearby recalls:

> We had one coal fire to heat the bungalow and the fuel could only be delivered in the summer. As a child I remember sitting on the front wall watching the delivery. It was my job to count that they delivered the correct number of sacks.

Some residents have also talked about the regular autumn job of cutting down the fast-growing bushes and trees in their plots to supplement the coal. If the coal ran out then there would be no possibility of getting another delivery. Marion Allwood from 'Eleanor' in Margaret Avenue noted that the local landscape would be transformed by this annual task. David Blaine explained that as a young man it was his job 'to cut logs for both fires on a sawing horse. I had two saws and one axe to split the logs.'

Coping with winter in the countryside was one of many challenges faced by hundreds of Londoners forced to flee their homes during the war. In the next chapter Peter will describe the conditions and tell their stories.

Chapter 12

Wartime Dunton

Relics from the Second World War still survive in the undergrowth around Dunton Hills. Foundations for Anderson shelters can still be found, with more complete structures at 'The Haven' and on the site of my family's 'Wendover' plot. Many were put to good use as storage sheds or other facilities by the ever-resourceful plotlanders when peace returned.

The war saw great changes for the plotlands and its population increased from 1939 onwards for a variety of reasons. Many of the plotlanders interviewed for this book moved to their weekend plots permanently at this time as a result of their homes in London being destroyed or simply and understandably to avoid the intense bombing. Being situated near the Thames estuary, important railway routes and close to London, they nevertheless found themselves under attack from the summer of 1940.

After the total defeat of the British army in Europe with its evacuation at Dunkirk, the German army seemed certain to arrive in Britain, by sea or air, with plotland homes situated on a very likely invasion route. Later, in the closing stages of the war, the V1 pilotless flying bomb and the V2 rocket caused death, injury and destruction as they landed short in the plotlands on the way to London from their continental launch sites. Plotlanders' memories give a flavour of those times.

Tom Wallace's family moved to a converted railway carriage in New Century Road after having experienced a miraculous escape from death when their house in Silvertown was hit by a landmine. For Tom it was a time of missed schooldays, evading the 'School Board' man on his bicycle by hiding in air-raid shelters. He recalls the image of German bombers flying low over treetops and being warned not to touch the 'butterfly bombs', small anti-personnel bombs designed to explode on touch.

Anne Wallace, Tom's future wife, was living at that time in Victory Avenue. A bomb dumped from an aircraft following the line of the railway lifted the roof off their bungalow which dropped back almost neatly into place, half an inch out of line. Her blind uncle, Fred Howard, was killed when he collided with a fallen

electricity cable and her cousin, Jimmy Howard, died with a friend when the cordoned-off landmine they had managed to approach suddenly exploded.

Alan Davies ('Lowlands', Raglan Road) recalls a schoolboy's fascination in watching the many dogfights that took place:

> I do remember that in the beautiful summer of 1940 the aerial fights were magnificent. Prior to radar, the Germans, bombing in daylight at this time, would find their way to targets in London by manually sighting on the Thames. We were no targets (except when they ditched their bombs) but they went right over us on their way to their targets. Of course, the RAF sought to intercept them before they reached their targets. The result was the most magnificent battle display one could ever hope to see. Parents and kids were all outside, peering up into the sky. Cheers went up when a German plane was seen to smoke and spiral downward. Groans would emanate when a Spitfire or Hurricane would turn to the earth in flames. On one occasion a German parachuted out of his stricken plane and headed earthward. Walking sticks, shovels, spades, were all gathered up as the old men and children (there were no young men; they were all gone to war) ran from place to place trying to be there when he landed.

Ron and Norman King outside the air-raid shelter of 'The Lens' in Victoria Road, 1943.

The poor chap, scared out of his mind no doubt, was confronted by a dozen spades and shovels as soon as his feet touched earth. No doubt he finished the rest of the war in fairly comfortable surroundings.

Possibly the pilot was taken to the nearby 'hutted' Prisoner of War Camp 266 at Dry Street in Langdon Hills.[1]

After being bombed out of the family home in Clapton, East London, the Firman family moved to 'Vera-Joan' in Hillcrest Avenue. Joan Firman was returning from work along Forest Glade one evening when the sounds of roaring aero engines and machine-gun fire in a dog-fight came so startlingly close that she dived into a muddy ditch to take cover. On another occasion, her father, Walter, watched a German airman bail out from his stricken fighter. Despite entreaties from his wife, Lucy, he went after the pilot with a garden fork, although the German landed miles away and Walter had to return without engaging the enemy.

During the period of the Blitz, Joan recalled seeing the dramatic fires reflected in the sky from London and the Thames installations, on one occasion finding the air filled with glowing and charred paper embers, carried by the wind from a bombed paper store somewhere near the Thames.

Sheila Mountfort's family had to move to 'Tetherdown' in Helmore Crescent because their own house in London was destroyed by a bomb. However, even moving to Helmore Crescent wasn't entirely safe, as Sheila explains:

A number of bombs dropped nearby and a V2 rocket hit the railway embankment next to our house. On another occasion a German plane crashed near Dunton Church and it unloaded its bombs before it crashed. One house in every three along Helmore Crescent ended up with a bomb in its garden.

Audrey Carter was living in 'Lilac' in Victory Avenue:

I remember my mother bathing my brother by the fire and of myself sitting at the table doing a jigsaw. I had just put in the last piece when a bomb dropped somewhere. The bungalow shook, the gas mantle fell down, my jigsaw broke up and Mrs Keen from 'Vera Villa' next door rushed in to see if we were all right!

Ron Crafer from Victoria Road remembers a bomb that dropped in the garden of the last bungalow in Dunton Drive behind the A.R.P. post next to the railway line, the bomber's probable target. This was a large bomb and produced a crater approximately 20 feet deep and 20 feet in diameter. The owner of the bungalow did not try to fill the crater, but instead decided to make a feature of it. He created a garden pond at the bottom with stepped walls at one foot intervals with a selection of plants. Ron thought that the whole design produced a very pretty effect.

Hornchurch aerodrome, the base for a succession of Spitfire squadrons of No. 11 Group, was a prime target. As part of its defence, a decoy airfield was laid out in fields off Doesgate Lane, between Langdon Hills and Bulphan. Remains of the more permanent features can still be seen today. Tended by six airmen, it would have had dummy installations – aircraft, vehicles, ammunition dumps, defensive positions – and, at night, fake runway lighting. On at least one occasion, it was successful in diverting the incendiaries and high explosives intended for Hornchurch.[2]

Barrage balloons were another familiar sight. Maureen Buck lived with her mother in 'Carlos' on the Lower Dunton Road, a small two-bedroom bungalow with living room and kitchen. Returning from a wartime overnight stay at Maureen's grandmother's house in Church Road, they were shocked to find their home wrecked and apparently looted. All the windows were broken, tiles from the roof were strewn in all directions around the garden and, inside, their furniture had been thrown around and was covered with splinters of shattered glass. Maureen recalls that according to their neighbour, Mrs Bonnett, a barrage balloon had escaped from its mooring and 'Carlos' had been in the path of the flailing cable. As a consequence they had to move to her aunt's place, 'St Elmo' on Lower Dunton Road.

The area also suffered from the V1 and V2 assault on London in the final stages of the war. Plotlanders would listen for the sound of a V1's engine cutting out prior to its final plunge to the ground and the subsequent explosion. One such rocket fell on Vowler Road and an ARP incident report of 14 November 1944 gives the following account:

> Vowler Road … approx. 50 casualties … 4 houses demolished completely, 5 seriously plus extensive minor damage … reserve and mobile units in action … military with mobile searchlights.[3]

Alan Davies remembers the same incident from a young boy's perspective:

> The rocket caused a huge but very localised pit which rapidly developed into a mini lake. Oddly, the only thing that survived intact was the bath tub. Within a few days or weeks, we lads had stuffed the drain of the bath tub with rags to stop the water seeping in and were sailing, or paddling rather, across the mini lake.

Ron Crafer recalls a small searchlight company that was stationed on the field at the corner of Church Road and Lower Dunton Road.

Dunton
Entertainment
Committee's
Accordion Band,
which entertained
troops at the
Searchlight Station.

He continues:

> This puzzled the public because by this later stage
> in the war there were few air raids by aircraft, only
> the V1 rockets, which could easily be seen. When the
> siren sounded, the searchlight was switched on, but
> remained stationary, shining directly upwards. No official
> explanation was given, but it was apparently one of a
> number of searchlights forming a ring around London.
> The general conception was that these lights were a guide
> for our own nightfighters. Once the V1 passed the arc of
> lights, no attempt was made to shoot it down.

Despite a buoyant 'Dunkirk spirit' and exciting sights and
sounds for schoolboys, the people of the area were under no illusions
about the constant danger they faced and the tragedies that occurred.
Helena Penny, Alice Shaw, Dorothy Mundy, Maude Simmons, and
her mother Charlotte Gladwin, were all killed when bombs were
dropped at Dunton on the night of 8 November 1940, devastating the
bungalow 'Veronica' on First Avenue and the immediate area.[4]

The Threat of Invasion
The RAF and Royal Navy would have made any direct attempt
at invasion an extremely hazardous undertaking for the Germans,
yet for the authorities the threat had to be regarded as a distinct

possibility for several years. Complex plans were made to counter an enemy attack in areas most at risk. The low-lying Essex coast, facing continental ports where barges and ships began to be concentrated, could well have been a potential target for a landing attempt. If the Germans had landed in the east or north-east of the county, the Basildon plotlands would very likely have been in the thick of the fighting, with the prepared defensive installations of the GHQ Line running from Chelmsford to Canvey Island to the east, the Thames Estuary defences to the south, and the last ditch Outer London Defence Ring to the west.[5]

Sir John Anderson is mainly remembered by later generations for the mass-produced air-raid shelter that bears his name, but he was responsible for other initiatives, too. In the House of Commons on 24 March 1942 Sir John unveiled the concept of the local Parish Invasion Committee (PIC):

> The duty of the committees is to survey their local problems, and to consider what might be their needs if fighting reached their district, how these needs can be met and how the civil and military authorities can best help each other.
>
> There are countless ways in which the help of civilians outside the organised services will be needed. In cooking and distributing food, for example, filling craters and shell-holes to enable military vehicles to pass, digging trenches, providing billets for troops moving in, or for neighbours bombed or shelled out. In a village or small town the invasion committee will be able to allot specific jobs to particular individuals; and most of the able-bodied inhabitants will know in advance what their role will be.[6]

In the Dunton/Laindon/Langdon Hills area, four such Parish Invasion Committees were set up, reporting back to a central Laindon group which in turn had representation in a wider group based on the Billericay area. This then formed part of the whole regional organisation. Records of the Dunton Committee have been preserved in the possession of the family of its chairman, Charles Leatherland, and give an interesting insight into the area at the time.

DO YOU KNOW WHAT TO DO——

IF GERMAN TROOPS REACH DUNTON?

We hope they will not get here. But if they should, the lives and welfare of us all may depend on whether proper plans have been made in advance to deal with the situation.

The

PARISH INVASION COMMITTEE

(officially constituted by order of the Regional Commissioner)

HAS NOT BEEN IDLE.

It has prepared, or is preparing, plans to deal with :—

Emergency Food Supplies	Welfare of Children
Residents Rendered Homeless.	Casualties
Water Reserves	Emergency Cooking
Gas Attacks	Defence Works

It is co-operating with the Police, Home Guard and Civil Defence Organisations.

The Committee is calling a

PUBLIC MEETING OF RESIDENTS

(Men, Women and Children)
to be held at

DUNTON ENTERTAINMENT HALL,

On Saturday, May 23rd——at 7 p.m.

The business of the meeting will be to :—

1—Hear a report from the Committee on what it has done and what it proposes to do.

2—Strengthen the Committee, and give it a more representative and democratic basis, by electing additional members from the Public Meeting.

We ask you to put aside your private engagements for this one evening, and regard it as one of the duties of good citizenship to attend.

CHARLES LEATHERLAND,
Chairman of the Invasion Committee.

THE " AYWUN " PRESS, LANGDON HILLS.

Poster advertising first PIC meeting, 1942.

Lord Leatherland

At this time, Charles Leatherland was developing an exceptional career in journalism, politics and public service that was to lead to an eventual life peerage under Harold Wilson in 1964 with the title of Baron Leatherland of Dunton. Among his many other honours, he was awarded the OBE for political and public service in 1951. A member of Essex County Council for 22 years, he was leader of the Labour group for 15 years and chairman of the council in 1960-1. He played a leading role in the establishment of the University of Essex, where he was awarded an honorary doctorate in 1973. He served as a magistrate for 26 years and became Deputy Lieutenant of Essex.

From humble origins in the Midlands, he had lied about his age in 1914 to join the Warwickshire Regiment, finishing the First World War as one of the army's youngest Company Sergeant Majors and decorated with the Military Medal. On leaving the army, he joined the Labour Party and became a founder member of the National Union of Ex-Servicemen, campaigning for the rights of the men returning from the war.

In 1921, Charles Leatherland began his career as a journalist, working for the *Macclesfield Courier*, where he rose to become chief reporter and sub-editor. Always an active and committed socialist,

Charles Leatherland.

he used his considerable journalistic skills during the General Strike of the 1920s to write a newsletter and major publications for the TUC. In 1929 he joined the staff of a national newspaper, the *Daily Herald*, as political sub-editor, becoming Assistant News Editor in 1938 and finally News Editor in 1941.[7]

In 1934 he purchased the substantial Old Rectory in Dunton. The property consisted of the house with six bedrooms and 20 acres of land with attached stables and a moat. He was an enthusiastic rider and supporter of the Dunton hunt and kept two or three horses. Generally he was regarded as having something of the status of the local squire, opening and attending local social events. Maureen Buck remembers seeing the grapes from Mr Leatherland's greenhouse adorning the pulpit for St Mary's harvest festival.

In 1951, Mrs Leatherland's health was giving some cause for concern and, on the advice of her doctor, the family moved to a smaller, more manageable house in Buckhurst Hill. Like many others, the family would have preferred to remain in Dunton, but left with cherished memories. Today, the Old Rectory has been transformed into a country hotel specialising in weddings.

The Dunton Parish Invasion Committee

At a public meeting on 23 May 1942, Charles Leatherland explained how the Dunton Parish Invasion Committee (PIC) had been formed and announced that he had been elected its chairman.

Meetings were held in the Church Hall, and minutes of the initial meetings in March 1942 show evidence of the energy and commitment of the local community in preparing its 'proper plans' in case 'German troops reach Dunton'. Lt. H.J. Poulten (Home Guard), the Military Representative, addressed the Committee concerning its status and duties. Again, he emphasised the importance of the local community's ability to organise its own resources and outlined the seriousness of situations that could develop. In the event of invasion, he would:

> assume command when he considers this is essential
> owing to:
> 1 – Approach of the enemy;
> 2 – State of panic among the civil population;
> 3 – Orders from a superior authority;
> 4 – Request of the civil authority.

Fulfilling Sir John Anderson's vision of empowering local expertise, the members of the initial committee took on duties as required, and members of the community who were in key occupations were invited to join, such as local farmers Mr Anderson, Mr Pigg and Mr Mountford (misspelling of Mountfort). The Reverend Isbister, rector of St Mary's, became co-ordinator of food supplies. Mr Lambert from 'Adastra' in Merrylands Road took over responsibility for first-aid provision.

The examples below show a number of key issues which were considered by the PIC. One of the first was the establishment of first-aid posts:

> Mr Lambert … reported that he had taken the following steps for the provision of a First Aid Post in Dunton Drive: Mrs Rongay [misspelling of Rungay] had mentioned to him that she had a building which she would be pleased for the committee to use. He added that the ARP authorities would provide equipment for the post at the Church Hall, and he thought he could obtain some equipment from the St John Ambulance Society for the post in Dunton Drive.[8]

Nurse Ada Rungay, 1940s.

Laindon Fire
Brigade, 1940s.

Inspector Carpenter, the police representative, raised the question of emergency cooking arrangements. A sub-committee was duly set up under the chairmanship of Mr Crutchley. 'Members: Mr Mudd, Mr Mountford, Mr Vickers, Mrs Vickers, Mrs Pratt, Mrs Rhomes, Mrs Thompson.'

On a more sombre note the Inspector raised the need to form plans for 'the burying of the dead' and agreed to arrange for a police lecturer to give guidance on precautions against poison gas. This was still considered a threat at the time to the extent that gas masks had been issued to the whole population from the outbreak of war. He continued by mentioning the alarm arrangements for an actual invasion, a sound that the committee no doubt hoped they would never hear: 'The Inspector announced that the ringing of the church bell in the event of invasion was a matter entirely for the Home Guard, and certain instructions had been issued.'[9]

Unsurprisingly, the availability of water for fire-fighting was also a concern, given the number of wooden buildings in the area:

> Mr Rogers put forward Dunton's demand for the provision of water tanks etc. for fighting fires in the unmade roads area. Mr Holmes, the Head Fire Guard for the four local areas, said that this matter was having his immediate attention.[10]

Documents provided by his grandson show that Charles Leatherland also wrote a personal account of one of the invasion committee meetings which helps to give a flavour of the atmosphere not possible to reproduce in official minutes. He begins:

> It is Friday. Eight o'clock. We are meeting in the village hall. There are planes up above. The night is damp and dismal. The trudge across the fields has been muddy. But the verger has stoked up a glowing fire. There are cups laid out in the corner. That promises a cheering cup of tea when our business is over. About 30 of us are present. We were elected as the Village Invasion Commitee a few months ago … we think we are fairly sensible and representative people.
>
> The Rector, as Food Officer, explains that the village's iron rations are now complete. 'They are safely stored, and the shopkeepers have all been told what they have to do from the moment the invasion bell rings in the old church tower.' He must keep details of his plans secret, but is sure they will work … [11]

Page 3 VICTORY AVENUE			Number of House	Men 16/65 Employed	Men 16/65 Unemployed	Women 16/65	Children	Invalids	A Local Defence Service Men	Money for...	Men for Trenches	Trained...	First Aid...	Recovery	Blankets	Mattresses	Sheets	Wells or Pond	Motor	S. Pump	Spades	Shovels	Picks	Wheelbarrows...	Experience...
NAME OF HOUSE	NAME OF HOUSEHOLDER	FURTHER PARTICULARS																						
ST ANNS	PAYNE		1	-	1	-	-	-	-	1	-	2	1	-	-	-	1	1	-	-	-	Y	Y
LOUISE																							
ST HELENA	CHARLTON	ST JOHNS AMB.	2	1	-	-	-	-	1	1	1	-	-	-	-	-	-	2	1	-	-	Y	Y
HAZELMERE	BONIFACE		5	2	-	1	2	-	-	2	1	Y	-	-	-	-	1	1	1	-	-	Y	Y
THE NOOK																							
WHITMORE																							
DAWN																							
ELM COTTAGE	WALDON	LONDON N.F.S	3	1	-	1	1	-	1	-	-	Y	-	-	-	W	-	2	1	-	-	Y	Y
OAK COTTAGE																							
SUNNYMEAD	MEGGS		2	-	-	2	1	-	-	-	-	-	-	-	W	-	-	-	-	-	Y	Y
MINNIE VILLA x	TAYLOR	SEE WHITE LODGE, TAYLOR REMOVED	2	-	-	1	-	-	-	1	-	-	-	-	W	-	2	2	1	1	-	Y	Y
RONALDENE	WINCH	WEEKEND BUNGALOW.																					
HOLMLEIGH	GIBBS		3	-	-	1	2	-	-	-	-	Y	-	-	W	-	-	-	-	-	-	Y	Y
AVONDALE	KEEN (SENIOR)		2	-	-	-	-	-	-	-	Y	Y	-	-	W	-	-	-	-	-	-	Y	Y
		BUNGALOW UNNAMED, SEE BERESFORD																					
VERA VILLA	KEENS		4	1	-	2	1	-	-	1	2	Y	-	-	Y	W	-	1	1	-	1	Y	Y
LILAC	FLACK		6	1	-	3	2	1	-	-	-	-	-	-	-	W	-	-	-	-	-	Y	Y
ST LEONARDS	JEFFERY		5	1	-	1	3	1	HG	-	1	-	-	-	-	-	-	-	-	-	-	Y	Y
ROSEMOUNT STORES	DREW (SENIOR)		2	-	Y	-	-	-	-	-	-	-	W	-	Y	1	1	-	1	-	Y	Y
DERRYDOWN	DREW		2	1	Y	1	-	-	-	-	-	-	W	-	-	1	1	1	-	-	Y	Y
ROSEDALE	CRUCHLEY	2 WOMEN 16/65, WEEKEND ONE ANNEXE, BUNGS, 3 CAMPS	2	-	-	-	-	-	-	-	-	-	W	-	1	1	1	1	-	Y	Y

The Dunton Parish Invasion Committee Survey, 1942

Page from PIC survey, 1942.

To help the committee to organise the resources of the area in terms of manpower, equipment and basic supplies, a questionnaire was circulated to every household. In those pre-computerised days, the results from the returned forms were recorded meticulously by hand in an exercise book, now in the possession of Mr Leatherland's grandson.[12]

The Dunton area covered 20 lanes on the north side of the railway including Victoria Road, Victory Avenue and Helmore Crescent, and surveys were completed by 258 properties which totalled 699 residents. Up to 80 per cent of properties were actively occupied and under six per cent specifically described as weekend bungalows, a proportion that reflects its importance as a wartime accommodation resource.

As a representative sample of the plotland area the survey highlights several interesting features. As far as employment was concerned, the survey's focus was on men between the ages of 16 and 65, reflecting the committee's conceptions of the nature of war work as well as contemporary assumptions regarding gender roles. Women, as expected, outnumbered the men at a time when many sons and younger partners had been called up and could well be serving overseas. Less than a third of the households contained male residents described as being employed in the area. Evacuation to the area, either as a precaution or out of actual necessity during the bombing of the London area, meant that many people were forced to commute to work using what public transport was available, predominantly the railway that had originally facilitated the development of the area. It was therefore important for the committee to have some idea of the extent of manpower available in the area at any time and a useful 59 per cent of the men reported a willingness to contribute to invasion defence duties.

Just under a third of households were prepared to accommodate the wounded and considering the limited nature of most plotland accommodation, as seen in the number of rooms and basic services, the mere 23 per cent of households willing to accept refugees could be regarded as an expected, if not encouraging, total.

An effective emergency water supply was a prime concern of the committee, who made preparations with the assistance of wider local authorities for treatment of water from wells and ponds. Only five households had mains water, and the 134 wells reflected the area's self-sufficient origins – now, ironically, a very useful wartime resource. The minutes of the Horndon-on-the-Hill PIC contain further information about water treatment procedure: '½oz bleaching powder to 100 gallons ... cover a sixpence for a bucketful (2 gals)'.[13]

The statistics also reveal the small number of cars (seven), lorries (one) and motor cycles (four) owned at the time, even allowing for properties with no return or judicious concealment of material facts.

An adequate stockpile of picks, shovels, spades (374) and wheelbarrows was available for the 108 men and 81 women who had reported as available for service, as well as the 27 stirrup pumps, although how effective these would have been against serious fire-bombing is a matter of conjecture.

The issuing of gas masks seems to have been successful, with various specific problems reported and dealt with. However, in particular details entered in the survey, there are some cases of residents who had stolidly refused to accept their respirator when offered.

'Exercise Mud'

It was not long before the organisation and preparations of the Dunton PIC were to be put to the test. On 28 September 1942, A.L. Seaman, the County Area Officer for Billericay and South Eastern Areas, sent letters to Mr Leatherland and the chairmen of the Laindon area PICs, informing them of a 'Combined Invasion Exercise to be held at Laindon on Sunday, 11th October 1942'.

This was given the code name 'Exercise Mud' and it presented a grim imaginary scenario:

General Narrative

The enemy has made a combined sea and airborne landing in the vicinity of Dovercourt and by the fourth day has established a bridgehead. A large force, despite strong resistance, has made steady progress and moved S.W. to the main London/Colchester road towards Chelmsford.

At the end of the fifth day, Chelmsford has fallen.

A thrust is being made S.W. to Brentwood via Ingatestone and similarly across Galleywood to Stock and Billericay with the apparent intention of reaching oil stores and the Thames.

Special Narrative

The Laindon Company of Home Guard has been at Action Stations since the first day of invasion.

At 07.00 hours on the 7th day, Brentwood has fallen and at 08.00 hours, Billericay is in enemy hands.

A force of 6 A.F.V's and approximately 200 lorried infantry are reported to be moving towards the fork road at Laindon Common, presumably to force a passage through the Laindon defences and open up the road towards the River Thames via Langdon Hills.

At 09.00/10.00 hours, Laindon, Dunton and Langdon Hills sustain heavy bombing by dive bombers using H.E. and I.B.'s [high explosives and incendiary bombs].

From reports of the enemy's movements on Laindon Common, it is apparent that an attack on Laindon from the N. is imminent.[14]

The Old Rectory owned by Charles Leatherland in the 1940s.

As chair of the PIC, Mr Leatherland was responsible for briefing members about the exercise and for ensuring that the public was made aware of the event. He emphasised that members 'will have to be on duty and carry out whatever work they are called on to do, just as they would in the event of a real invasion'. His briefing notes set out the various duties and the methods of communication with the Committee's HQ at the Old Rectory. He also suggested that before the 'battle' began the Area Leaders should:

> have a private word with half a dozen neighbours each, and have those neighbours willing to be put 'on tap' if they are needed. That will be much better than trying to 'commandeer' them officially during the battle.

He also reminded members that between 9.00 a.m. and 10.00 a.m. they should keep under cover as 'the whole district is supposed to be heavily dive bombed. If Committee officials expose themselves, umpires may declare them casualties. That will upset our working plans.'[11]

The whole exercise was to last for 4½ hours from 'stand to' at 8.00 a.m. to 'stand down 'at 12.30 p.m. with 'action stations' at 9.00 a.m. The roles of attackers and defenders were carried out by home guard members with 'E' company acting as the defending force. As a guide to recognition, the defenders were to wear 'field service caps with flaps down'. The attacking force was initially to have worn steel helmets, but this was later changed to 'woollen cap comforters'. 'Fifth columnists' were not to be used on this occasion.

Umpires were responsible for assessing the effectiveness of the various participants and, in addition, 'incidents' would be created to put the local preparations to the test: 'Umpires will initiate incidents with thunderflashes and other effects. Civil Defence Umpires will be responsible for making military casualties.'

The exercise was designed to test each of the local services as well as their ability to work together: home guard and Air Raid Protection (A.R.P.) Warden preparedness, effectiveness of communications, fire-fighting by the National Fire Service and street fire parties, treatment of casualties, emergency food distribution, transfer of corpses to the mortuary and maintenance of water supplies.

The local members of the Dunton Parish Invasion Committee were allocated the following roles:

> **At committee headquarters**: Mr Leatherland, Mr Pigg, P.C. Page, motor cycle messenger.
> **Liaison with Civil Defence**: Mr Blackaby.
> **Area leaders:** No. 1 Area – Mr and Mrs Cook, Mrs Noakes; No. 2 Area – Mr and Mrs Vickers; No. 3 Area – Possibly Mr Wilson; No. 4 Area – Mr Crafer, Mrs Pratt, Mrs Mudd; No. 5 Area – Mr Embrey, Mrs Emeny, Mrs Floyd.
> **Food and Rationing**: The rector, Rev. Isbister.

The exercise duly took place on 11 October and a report produced. Mr A. Vickers, leader of No. 2 Area, describes how his team reacted to events:

> I received a verbal message from Warden Blackaby for a Fire Squad to report to Dunton School at 11 o'clock and three men were dispatched at 11.15 with 1 stirrup pump, 2 pails and long handed shovels.
>
> When I was at First Aid Post later, a message received that Dunton Colony had been bombed and we have casualties. I made preparations for refugees if needed.[11]

A young Ron Crafer, son of the leader of No. 4 Area, was assigned to Mr Leatherland as a messenger equipped with his bicycle. He remembers being told to take a report to the Laindon Report Post concerning a crashed aircraft on the Arterial Road that had broken into two halves. For the purpose of the exercise, two cars had been set on fire and the road was closed for several hours. Ron says the 'considerable air activity', intended to represent intensive German dive bombing attacks, was provided by what he regarded at the time as extremely ancient biplanes, painted yellow.

In his assessment of 'Exercise Mud' for the County Area Officer, Mr Leatherland was pleased to report that: 'Our arrangements generally speaking worked very smoothly.' He had evidently appreciated the resource of Ron Crafer on his bicycle as, drawing attention to difficulties encountered on the day, such as problems of effective communication, he states: 'On another occasion, I had two messages waiting to go from my H.Q. to Report Centre for 20 minutes, and as the DR (dispatch rider) had not returned to me, I had to utilise cycle messengers.'

Mr Leatherland was later invited to act as an umpire for 'Exercise Dust' involving the Grays Parish Invasion Committee.

Life must go on

Despite air raids and threats of invasion, life had to go on. Ivy King, whose family moved to Railway Approach around 1928, shared memories of her wartime wedding:

> We got married in St Nicholas Church. I had to walk down Durham Road – an unmade road – to the car. Good job it was a dry day as white satin dress and wellington boots don't go very well. For the reception we had the British Legion Hall which was a long way from our house. Mum was able to get some 'under the counter' meat as it was 1941 and rationed. Many local folk gave things to help out. On the morning of the wedding, a bridesmaid and myself put all the food in a pram to take

Marjory Earle's 'Earlettes'. The group was formed to raise funds for the war effort.

it to the hall. Half the journey was on unmade road. From time to time we would get stuck in a rut, over spill the food, brush it off and go on our way again. Still, a lovely time was had by all. It was late September so got dark early. The hall did not have blackout blinds so we all walked to a club about a mile or so away to finish the feast and have a drink. Still in our wedding clothes we made our way home to the end of Durham Road about 11 p.m. all singing an old song called 'When the Lights go on in London'.

The Dunton School Log Book, maintained by headteacher Mr L. Newman, gives an evocative impression of local school life under wartime conditions.[15] It reports that on 28 September 1938, the day on which the British Fleet was mobilised during the tense period of Neville Chamberlain's negotiations with Hitler for 'peace

135

in our time', an evening meeting was held with parents to discuss instructions sent to the school concerning 'what action should be taken in the event of an outbreak of hostilities'. However, by 1 October 'the suggested evacuation of children … has been cancelled'.

VE Day Party on Third Avenue. 19 May 1945. Mrs Folkerd ('Violet Lodge') stands on the left.

On 4 September 1939: 'Owing to the declaration of a state of war between England and Germany, the school is closed for a further week … ' When the school eventually reopened on 2 October only 15 pupils were present and that week's total attendance amounted to only 17.6 per cent of a total school roll of 98 pupils. Local residents seemed to have grown accustomed to the new circumstances, however, and attendance rose at the start of the new term on 2 January 1940 to 47 present. By 18 June, with the Battle of Britain increasing in intensity, Mr Newman could note: 'Enemy air activity over this district last night … Attendance has fallen today from 93 per cent to 68 per cent.'

On 14 June 1940, the school's air-raid shelters had been completed. As the German bombing campaign increased, daily routine was frequently interrupted by alerts throughout the autumn of 1940. For 15 November alone, Mr Newman recorded three alerts during the day: 9.10 – 10.06; 10.38 – 11.00; 13.15 – 14.10. He also noted that: 'a number of bombs fell in the village last weekend. This coupled with bad weather has caused a slump in attendance.'

Audrey Carter recalls that: 'During raids that occurred while we children were at Dunton School, we sang songs in the shelter to keep our spirits up.' The school continued to provide some light relief for pupils in other ways, and on 12 December 1940 the log showed: 'A very enjoyable Christmas party was held this afternoon.'

As the war dragged on, the school helped the children to become involved in the various civilian campaigns. In 1943, the school collected 1,800 books in four days for the Salvage Book Drive on 20 April, and on 21 May 1944 pupils saved £36 during the 'Salute the Soldier' savings week.

During the early summer of 1944, young Joe Cotterill and his friends watched the build up of troops and equipment before D-Day. Flying bombs became an increasingly disruptive problem from the middle of June until the school closed for the summer holidays on 4 August, with a total of 67 recorded alerts. For example:

> June 27th: Owing to strong winds, it has not been possible to hear the Laindon siren all day. The Report Post omitted to phone the 1.10 p.m. all clear so the children were in the shelters the whole afternoon up to 3.33 p.m. (closing time).

> July 11: Alerts: 9.19 – 9.43; 11.18 – 12.36; 12.52 – 1.37; 2.35 – 3.39pm. Managers' meeting this afternoon.

Difficulties continued into the new school year when the school canteen sustained minor damage after a V1 was shot down onto the A127 on 24 September. During the whole of November until 13 December the school had no central heating owing to a boiler failure necessitating transfer of classes into the headmaster's room, the teachers' room and the canteen.

1945 saw further challenges with overflowing cesspools that were to be a thorn in Mr Newman's side for the rest of the school year:

> March 13: The three cesspools were emptied this morning. The contractor reported to me after he had finished the work and I then found that the contents had been pumped out on to the playing field.

Finally, on 8 May 1945, 'School closed for three days to celebrate the end of hostilities in Europe.'

The Crafers' wedding at St Mary's, Dunton, in 1953. Some of our contributors are included. Left to right: the Rev. Isbister, Peter Ellis, Sheila Galpin, Ron and Georgie Crafer, Alice White, ?, Freddie Peck, Joe Cotterill (Goodman).

Chapter 13

A Portrait of the Local Community

As Peter showed in the previous chapter, the Dunton plotland population grew rapidly during the war and the local community had to be flexible enough to cope with the changes. Residents recalled that there was a lively sense of community for those permanent residents who didn't want to keep themselves to themselves. Peter Ellis, whose family lived in 'St Elmo', on Lower Dunton Road between Third and Fourth Avenues, explained that:

> The community focused around a number of organisations: the local school, the Sunday School, the Choral League, the Church, the Local Amateur Dramatics Group (The Revellers), the Entertainment Committee, the Fur and Feather Club and various youth groups like the Scouts. The Sunday School was held by Miss Cruchley, who was very active and organised many outings for the locals. Even when she was over 80 she was still holding Sunday School.

The Dunton School
The local school was clearly an important feature of the community. Situated on Lower Dunton Road, Dunton School was the primary school attended by most of the local plotland children. *Kelly's Directory* from 1922 notes that the school was built in 1843 for 31 children.[1] In the 1930s, as the size of the local population was growing with the arrival of the plotlanders, a new school was built a few hundred yards down the road and the old school closed. During the 1930s and 1940s, when the local population was reaching its peak, its roll fluctuated between 94-123 pupils.[2] However, as the population fell in the late 1970s the school finally shut its doors with only 12 pupils left on its roll.[3] During its 40-year life its heads included Elsie Curzon (1929-36), Mr Newman (1936-49), and Mrs Mazonowicz in the late 1960s.

A library van also visited the school regularly in the 1930s, providing a service to the local community as well as the school. The School Log from 1932 notes that there were 171 members of the library including 49 children.[4]

Nina Humphrey recounts her mother's memories of the old school in the 1920s:

My mother, and later her brothers, were enrolled at Dunton School in Lower Dunton Road which they accessed by walking across several fields from Alexandra Road which was pleasant enough in summer, but not so in winter due to the mud. The little village school, which had few amenities, was, however, run by an excellent Governess who taught a mixed class of children. My mother held her in high regard, and missed her when she had to take two weeks off work with the 'flu. The class was taken to Ingrave School for the duration, which had better facilities including a netball court, but the children were happy to return to Dunton once their teacher had recovered.

Jean Dallinger, who lived in Merrylands Road, attended the school in the 1940s and recalls the walk through the unmade plotland lanes:

Children from the area (including some of my relatives) would group together to walk to and from school. Often I went with my cousin who was a dinner lady there. There were two routes to school: one along the cinder track, and the other along Merrylands Chase. The school took children up to the age of 11 and there were three classes: infants, juniors, seniors. I remember the headmaster, Mr Newman, was a formidable man who taught the seniors and ran the school choir. The other two teachers were women. As part of the choir we would enter local festivals.

Audrey Carter, who was living in Victory Avenue, gives her memories:

It was a small school with only three classrooms, one of which was divided by a screen. Although we were only small I can remember one year we won the district sports and the music festival. We practised our scales and spent before school and playtimes skipping. As a reward for our efforts our headmaster Mr Newman treated us to a coach outing to London Zoo.

Our school dinners were cooked by Mrs Dunstan and Mrs Overy and served in the Village Hall that was next to the school. One day, on arrival we were surprised and shocked to find that the hall had burnt down! From then on our dinners were brought in from Laindon School and served in the classrooms with the screen rolled back.

Rose Cousins (*née* King), who lived in 'Haystacks', a former poultry farm on Lower Dunton Road near the junction with Stack

Dunton School, 1930s. Kenneth Newberry, of Second Avenue, is one of the pupils.

Avenue, attended the school during the war when Mr Newman and two female teachers, Mrs Gray and Miss Craswell, were working there. She remembers being paid 3d. per lb by the school to pick rosehips to be turned into rosehip syrup. Incidentally, when she was a little older Mrs Cousins remembers someone called Mr Denny who lived in a property on the Southend Arterial Road paying local children to collect a wild flower that grew in the area. She called it the kissing herb because parts of its yellow flower would get stuck to their clothes as they gathered it. He would arrive with his horse and cart to collect it and paid 15 shillings for a hundredweight. She thought the plant was being used in the chemical or pharmaceutical industry.

Peter Ellis was also enrolled at the school, but admits that he wasn't a keen attender and could remember visits from Mr Mitchell, the School Board man.

Compared with schools today, it appears that Dunton School had a much wider involvement in local affairs. The Head's log from July 1931 describes how she had to deal with the case of three local boys who were accused of stealing. They admitted having 'broken open the box of money on Durham Road – the path fund – after going to the pictures on Saturday'. The parents agreed 'to thrashing at school instead of taking the case to court … with the children to pay it back'. Mr Davidson, representing the Path Fund Committee, accepted this resolution of the matter.[5] I guess that's one alternative to issuing an ASBO!

Shopping
There was a number of small shops in the plotlands, often run from residential premises. When the Dunton Hills Estate was designed, plots on the corners where the Avenues met Hillcrest and Central Avenue were earmarked for shops. In reality only one was used for this purpose. That was the Henderson's 'Top Shop' at the top of First Avenue. Contrary to its nickname, it had nothing to do with trendy clothing. The Hendersons also ran a post office and stores on Lower Dunton Road between First and Second Avenues.

On the estates to the west of Laindon several shops get a mention, including Rosemount Stores in Victory Avenue, which was run by the Drews in the 1940s and 1950s, and Invicta Stores at the Dunton end of Worthing Road. In the 1970s I can remember going to a small shop on Lower Dunton Road near the school, and also making regular walks down to the shop on Dunton caravan site. Neither survives today.

Many people lament the loss of the shops in Laindon High Road, and more than one person has contrasted its fate with that of nearby Billericay High Street, which managed to keep its shops. In its heyday of the 1930s and 1940s, Laindon and its mile-long High Road was booming, with nearly 200 commercial businesses listed for the town, many of them shops. However, with the building of Basildon the town began to change dramatically. In the late 1950s there were still around a hundred shops running along either side of Laindon High Road. The Corporation noted that the construction of Basildon town centre would affect the shops in Laindon and in its 1955 annual report it noted that: 'The Chamber of Commerce and the Corporation are agreed that redevelopment on modern lines is necessary in view of the likely competition.'[6] Their plans came to fruition when a new grey concrete Laindon Shopping Centre was opened in 1969.[7] Interestingly, sections of it were demolished in 2008 and the rest is earmarked for redevelopment in the next few years.

Nina Humphrey notes that, in the days before fridges or freezers, shopping was a very regular routine:

> In the 1950s supermarkets hadn't yet arrived so a shopping trip would involve visiting individual shops for individual items. We'd get meat from the butchers (Sizer's or Buckingham's); bread from Cottis's; other food from the grocers (Sloper's or Green's) or the Co-op, which had the overhead system of transporting the cash to the office in little cups on pulleys; toiletries from Wilson's chemists; newspapers and sweets from Boon or Weeden's; clothes from the various haberdashers, Violet Butler's or Henbest's; and shoes from Bata and Curtis where I had my feet measured for school shoes which involved sliding my feet into what seemed to be an X-ray machine!
>
> Pelham's was our nearest sweetshop. Mrs Pelham was a little elderly Jewish woman, quiet, astute and always dressed in black clothes trimmed with black lace. The shop was dark and dreary and a curtain hung in the doorway at the back from where Mrs Pelham would appear when the shop doorbell rang. As well as sweets, Mrs Pelham also sold penny drinks. She kept some shot glasses alongside some bottles of fizzy cordial. If we asked for a penny drink, she would take the top off the bottle, fill the shot glass and replace the bottle top tightly, then hand us the shot glass in exchange for our penny. She would wait while we drank it and then take the glass from us. That was my first taste of a fizzy drink, as at that time

we had only ever had squash at home. I thought it was absolutely delicious, sheer nectar after a long walk home from school on a hot summer afternoon. Apparently if you asked for a tuppenny drink she would half fill a tumbler. Unfortunately I was never that flush.

My mum would go shopping on her bike and bring the groceries home in bags hanging from the handlebars. Most women in Laindon would shop daily and walked with their home-made shopping trolleys from their plotland homes down to the shops. These trolleys came in a variety of shapes and sizes, most had pram wheels attached, some had lids. Some were natural wood, some were painted bright colours. My nan knew lots of women in the village, and she also knew each of them by their shopping trolley. If we saw a trolley parked outside a shop, she would say: 'Lizzy [from 'Woodhams' in Alexandra Road] must be shopping in there, because her trolley's parked outside.'

The Victory Stores and Deliveries

For those who couldn't make the long walk to the shops, there was always the possibility of having shopping delivered. Peter Jackson used to work as a delivery boy for the Victory Stores, run by the Lungleys, in Berry Lane at the junction with Bridge Road. In the 1970s the shop was known to me simply as 'Jim's shop' as it was then run by Jim Robertson and his wife, Joan. The shop has now gone, but Peter recalls what it was like making deliveries to the plotlands:

> The Victory Stores, situated at the junction of Bridge Avenue and Berry Lane, had been an important convenience store and amenity centre for the local area, formerly run by a Mr Townsend and later by Mr and Mrs George Lungley. The local pillar box stood outside the shop and to one side was a telephone kiosk, very important in the days when not everyone had the benefit of their own connection and mobile phones were still in the realms of science fiction.
>
> Lungley's shop was well patronised by the permanent residents of the Berry Lane area, but also benefited from trade from the plotlanders who regularly passed on their way from Laindon Station to the Dunton Hills Estate. Its

Lungley's shop on Berry Lane, 1966.

importance was even greater after Mr Cockshaw closed his shop further along Berry Lane at the corner with Lincewood Park Drive. In addition, the Victory Stores continued to offer a delivery service to all local areas, carried out by a succession of local lads and an old trade bike.

This bicycle was a venerable piece of equipment by the time I took my turn on its saddle in the mid-1960s. It had a small front wheel under a large carrying box at the front and a metal frame for goods over the back wheel behind the saddle. Rod brakes, battery lamps front and back and no gears completed the specification.

In view of the customer base, a good local knowledge, especially of the plotland area, was an important qualification for the job. Years of wandering around the area, knowledge of the location of properties and experience of cycling on the narrow concrete paths made me a candidate for the job. Other plotland residents held the post, too. Joe Cotterill, brought up on Hillcrest Avenue, worked for the Victory Stores in the years around 1954. His friend, Ken Page, who lived in Ronald Avenue, took over from Bruce Bellamy when he left school in 1958 and Stefan Labedzki took over from him the next year. Ron Ashton from 'Hawthorn' in Berry Lane made deliveries for Cockshaw's shop.

Paraffin was a common plotland fuel for heating, lighting and, sometimes, cooking. Ken remembers George Lungley carefully and laboriously filling the large metal cans with paraffin, quart by quart in a measuring jug, sometimes two, four, or five gallon cans, for the front of the bike and one behind. This would provide supplies for the week for a plotland household. In winter, the characteristic smell of paraffin heating would often waft out of a bungalow when the door was opened to receive a delivery. The delivery boy could also smell of paraffin, especially when the cap on the can carried in the rear pannier was a loose fit and sprayed drops of the fuel over his back when going over the many bumps. Sometimes a customer would order a bag or bags of coal, which were loaded either on the front or back of the bike. Limited food storage facilities in plotland properties meant that tins were very popular, as well as crown-capped bottles of sterilised milk that would keep all week, sometimes ordered by the crate.

The bike itself was quite heavy, and when fully loaded with paraffin, coal or large cardboard boxes of groceries, it took a fair amount of skill to negotiate the

Peter in his delivery outfit, outside 'Wendover' in 1965.

plotland lanes. Progress along the narrow concrete paths was generally satisfactory, although you had to be on your guard against meeting other people coming in the opposite direction, especially around blind corners such as the corner of Forest Glade and Beech Hall Gardens. Strength and skill were required for keeping a straight line when climbing an incline. Problems arose at the end of these paths when the mud was at its wettest. The only way forward was to dismount and push your way through the mire and standing water. Summer, when the land dried out, and sharp frosts in winter that froze the mud solid, created golden times when you could keep pedalling. However, anyone who did the job throughout the year will remember the many Friday evenings and Saturdays pushing that trade bike through the mud with pelting rain and sodden clothes.

The hills that created much of the attraction of the plotlands were a mixed blessing to the delivery boy. The first was the upward slope of Berry Lane, past New Avenue. I never improved on my record of getting up to Shakespeare Avenue without having to push. The downward slope of Forest Glade was a gift for the loaded outward journey, not too bad returning empty. The more extreme incline of the southern end of Hillcrest Avenue, known as 'The Dip', provided a certain exhilaration going down at speeds the bike was never designed for – but it had to be paid for coming back up.

'The Dip' had a concrete path, but the rest of Hillcrest Avenue on the way to Sunnyside Gardens or Margaret Avenue was without any hard surface. In fact, it still retained the undulations dating from ploughing when it was agricultural land. When the surface was solid enough, this gave a pleasant up and down merry-go-round move-ment on the descent from the top of Fourth Avenue to Third Avenue, but became something of a nuisance when negotiating the less favourable section to the top of Second Avenue. From just past the dustbins at the top of Forest Glade, the return to the Victory Stores down the long hill along Berry Lane gave a welcome relief with minimal effort.

Accidents, however, could and did happen. Standing on the pedals to keep moving uphill under load could be risky on the old bike when the chain was loose and liable to slip suddenly, making you lose control with painful results. On one occasion I had two deliveries to make. A crate of 12 bottles of sterilised milk had to be left in the front box while I propped the bike up against a telegraph pole to deliver a box of groceries from the pannier at the back. Perhaps it was the strong wind blowing at the time or the loose mud under the tyres or the small wheel doing its trick of turning unexpectedly under the uneven weight from the front that did it. While I was yards away from the bike, I had to watch as it leaned over in slow motion and fell to the ground, covering the mud and grass with sterilised milk and broken glass.

The Dip at the end of Hillcrest Avenue, 1960s.

Ken Page remembers some incidents he experienced:

> I did crash once going down the Glade, up-ended the lot in the mud. I think the groceries were for the Hayballs in Beech Hall Gardens. I had to take them back and clean them up and go out again. The Lungleys weren't very impressed but it was my only prang in my year or so there. The handlebars broke off one day and I ended up in the ditch up near the dustbins. I had to carry the bike back to the shop then George went and got some new ones and we fitted them.

Other Delivery Services

The other important delivery service was provided by the milkman. Maureen Buck's father, Jim Downs, took over the milk round from Mr Sloper's 'Sunnymede Stores' in Laindon after he returned from active service in the war. Maureen Buck's family were long-standing residents of Dunton. Her grandmother, Mrs Downs, had been the sexton at St Mary's church and her grandfather had been the head cowman at Anderson's Farm.

Maureen remembers her father servicing an extensive round throughout the year with his horse and cart, which was often the only way of negotiating the unmade roads. Sometimes Maureen would accompany her father as he picked up the horse and cart from the stable in Victoria Road and collected his day's load from Markham's Dairy. She would then help him deliver his bottles, which in those days included a quart size as well as the familiar pint.

On one occasion, Maureen said, he was working at the northern end of Hillcrest Avenue when the conditions were so bad that the axle broke on the cart. A local resident had married a former German P.O.W. who had been imprisoned at the old army camp on Church Road. By coincidence he had been a blacksmith by trade and took matters in hand. He lit a fire close by, helped to unload the milk from the cart and, with his bellows and improvised blacksmith's tools, repaired the damage on the spot. It was a great relief to Jim to be able to continue his round.

Maureen remembers Jim stubbornly working in all weathers, even when he wasn't well. While serving in the Far East he had contracted malaria, and suffered from recurrent shivering attacks due to latent malaria for the rest of his life. He was a regular visitor to Dr Chowdhary in Laindon, who had instantly recognised his problem.

As the New Town grew, the plotlands declined and so did the demand for the milk delivery service. In 1965 the Sunnymede Stores horse-drawn milk service came to an end with the sale of the whole business and Jim went back to the building trade he had known before the war. The Slopers finally emigrated to Australia.

Peter Ellis remembers a winkle man visiting the Dunton Estate regularly, and an accumulator man who would collect accumulators for recharging. The coalman would be a regular sight, but only in the summer months, as it was impossible to get up the hill in the winter.

Milk delivery to the plotlands from the Richards' Farm at the end of King Edward Road.

Medical Services

When land agents first started to sell plots of land around Laindon they waxed lyrical about the delights of the area. Among the reasons to move there was the fact that it was such a healthy place that it did not even have a local doctor. Now that's what I call spin.

As the population grew, there was clearly a need for a local doctor. Dr Shannon took up the post from 1913, but there is one doctor, Dr Chowdhary, whose name is often mentioned with affection by local residents. He even had a local school named after him. He came to Laindon in 1931 from the Punjab region of India and soon settled into his new life. Making house calls to plots on unmade roads must have made the job very difficult at times, but would have allowed the doctor to see the poor conditions in which some residents were living. George Ross notes that, in the days when people had to pay for visits and medicine, Dr Chowdhary would often not charge the very poorest for his services.[8]

Nina Humphrey gives her memories of visiting Dr Chowdhary in the 1950s:

> His surgery was in a house called 'Daisybank' in Laindon
> High Road and the waiting room was the front living room.
> I don't think there was an appointment system. We simply
> arrived at 9 a.m., the receptionist would come in, take our
> names and then we would wait our turn. After a few minutes
> we would hear a rush of water. My mother told me: 'That's
> Dr Chowdhary's bath water running away – he always takes
> a bath before surgery.' Dr Chowdhary's practice was joined
> by Dr Ruby and, later, Dr Martin and Dr Cavaroli.

George Ross mentions that Dr Martin and Dr Cavaroli spoke at the Public Inquiry in October 1975 which was called to consider Basildon Development Corporation's South West Area Plan. He noted that the two local doctors 'were a credit to the town in that they gave long statements and stood up very well under cross-examination by Mr Boniface'.[9]

Pat Jackson's parents moved to 'Albermary', which was in Worthing Road at the corner with Dunton Drive, to be closer to relatives who owned several plots in Helmore Crescent. She remembers the local midwife, Nurse Pond, who travelled the area on her bike:

> Nurse Pond helped to deliver my younger brother on the
> same day as she had delivered twins for a gypsy family,
> who were camped up for winter in their wooden caravan
> nearby in a copse off Brentwood Road. When she told my
> mother how tiny the twins were my mother asked her to
> pass on the baby clothes that she had bought for her own
> baby. He had been expected to be tiny, but turned out to
> be a ten-pounder.

Entertainment

Those who wished to watch the latest blockbuster could visit the Radion Cinema, which stood at the junction of Laindon High Street and New Century Road. Screenings of films were sometimes also shown in Dunton Church Hall, and Rose Cousins remembers the amusement when the film would stop abruptly and a whip-round would hastily be organised to raise money to feed the electricity meter. Occasionally films would also be shown from the back of a lorry in the school grounds.

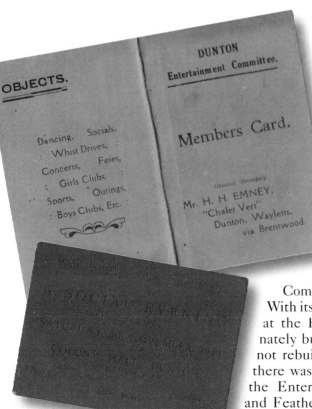

The Entertainment Club and the Fur and Feather Club memorabilia.

Those inspired to act after watching their on-screen heroes and heroines, or who felt the need to act out scenes they had missed when the meter had run out, could join the local amateur dramatics group 'The Revellers', or one of the local dance groups. The Crafers from Victoria Road remember Marjory Earles' 'Earlettes' being a popular group in the war when it helped to raise funds for the forces.

The Dunton Entertainment Committee organised local entertainment. With its resident accordion band it was based at the Entertainment Hall, which unfortunately burnt down in the late 1940s and was not rebuilt due to lack of funds. Apparently there was a certain degree of rivalry between the Entertainment Committee and the Fur and Feather Club, but one Christmas the two groups pooled their rationed supplies to hold a joint Dinner and Dance.

The Dunton Fur and Feather Club

The community was rural at heart with several residents recalling how they used to help on local farms at harvest time. Many plotlanders owned their own poultry and animals, so it is not surprising that there was an active local Fur and Feather Horticultural Society. In 1948 it had around 330 members.[10]

Its annual summer show was a chance for locals to display the pick of their crops, poultry and rabbits. The 1946 show leaflet gives a good idea of the range of produce which was being grown locally, with prizes advertised for a wide variety of salads and vegetables, including shallots, beet, cabbage, beans, peas and potatoes. David Blaine's parents and grandparents lived in Sidney Road and were regular winners at the annual shows. They proudly collected dozens of cups and trophies.

As well as regular horticultural competitions, the club also organised many social events and outings. Its first Annual Dinner Dance was held on 9 November 1946. Rose Cousins recalls it often held these events in one of the halls on the old farm Colony. The site of the Colony is now the Dunton Caravan Park.

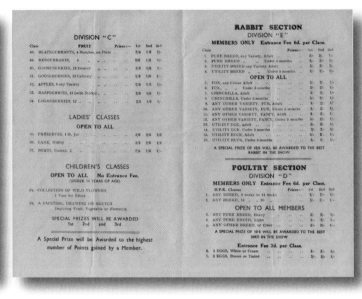

Show programme for the Dunton Fur and Feather Club, 1946.

A Plotland Childhood

We couldn't finish a chapter about the strength of the local community without briefly telling Joe Goodman's story. In many ways it embodies the plotland spirit and shows the power of a local community to sustain its members.

Joe Cotterill, as he was known as a child, was found abandoned in a pram outside Churchill and Johnson builders' merchants near Laindon Station in 1939. He was immediately taken in by Ethel Thomas who lived in 'Clearview' on Hillcrest Avenue. The Thomases fostered a number of children, and during his childhood Joe spent time living in different properties around the Dunton Hills Estate and attended the local Dunton School. He recalls his teacher

Inspecting the produce. Dunton Fur and Feather Club, 1940s.

asking him on a number of occasions whether he had moved again. Joe took a full part in local activities and he pops up in many photos from the 1940s as a church bell-ringer, attending coach outings and attending the VE Day party on Third Avenue. He also helped with making tea and producing posters for the Fur and Feather Club and took his turn as a delivery boy for the Victory Stores.

Joe went on to have a very successful career as a professional comedian, winning 'Opportunity Knocks' in the 1970s, being in 'The Comedians', and appearing at Royal Variety Shows. Attending the regular reunions, he often keeps his plotland friends entertained by delivering great stand-up routines. I found it delightful to watch him interact with visitors at an event Peter and I held at the Langdon Reserve to record peoples' memories and photographs. His easy manner and memories of living in so many places meant that he was able to glide round the room helping to gel other peoples' stories together. It strikes me that he is an embodiment of the enduring plotland spirit!

Coach outing from the Fur and Feather Club, 1948.

View of the scattered development on
the Dunton Hills Estate seen from
'Vera-Joan' in the late 1930s.

PART TWO

THE END OF THE PLOTLANDS

Members of the Laindon Residents' Protection Association in 1977. Left to right: George Ross Snr, A. Davison, George Ross (Chair and author of *Brink of Despair*),Stan Hollands, Charles Wright and Ray Popkin.

Chapter 14

The New Town Cometh

As well as hearing from plotlanders we also wanted to give a voice to Basildon Development Corporation, as it played such a major role in the story of the plotlands. Extracts from its archives give an indication of how this body went about the task of creating a town which, according to Lewis Silkin, the Minister of Town & Country Planning, 'people from all over the world will want to visit'.[1]

Going through Essex Record Office's huge collection of Corporation files was quite a journey of discovery for me. Bear in mind that my childhood prejudices had painted the Corporation as some kind of evil empire intent on stealing away 'Halliford', my happy holiday home, and replacing it with concrete monstrosities, with all the charm of nuclear fall-out shelters. Many other residents felt similarly.

However, I must confess that as I ploughed through the vast number of documents in the Corporation's files, the administrator in me became amazed by the achievements of the staff and the huge task they were facing. The files revealed the difficult course the Corporation had to steer between many, often competing, demands: the 'requests' emanating from successive ministers with responsibility for Town and Country Planning (all of whom had their own political agendas to serve); the concerns of the local population whose plots were earmarked for development and who were naturally anxious about what the new town meant for them; the frustration of the existing local council which could see some of its own plans for house-building stymied by the constraints of the Master Plan; the pressure to meet the needs of the London boroughs who wanted homes for those on their waiting lists who had been displaced during the war; and the practical problems that inevitably arose during such a major construction project. Soap operas have been written using less material!

It was just a pity, I reflected, remembering all the little 'shacks' that had disappeared one by one, that there had been no room in the Master Plan for those who wanted alternative ways of living.

The New Town is Announced
The fate of the plotlands was sealed in the late 1940s with the passing of two significant Acts of Parliament which directly affected

155

the local community: the 1947 Town and Country Planning Act, which severely curtailed unregulated development, and the 1946 New Towns Act, which gave the regulatory framework for the establishment of Basildon New Town.

New towns were needed to cope with the urgent need for housing in the post-war period as the population began to grow. A lack of building during the war coupled with the destruction of many homes meant that there was a major housing shortage. In the plotlands around Laindon and Pitsea thousands of people were living in what the authorities saw as substandard housing. Billericay Council therefore pushed for the creation of a new town as it saw this as an excellent way of getting funds and external support to deal with this mass of substandard housing within its boundary.

Basildon Development Corporation (BDC) was not established until February 1949, but before it came into being the hornets' nest had already been stirred. Once Basildon was announced as one of the 'New Towns', there was naturally a great deal of confusion and anxiety spreading through the existing community in Laindon and Pitsea. On 30 September 1948 the Minister for Housing, Lewis Silkin, came to Laindon to address a meeting of local residents and explain what was planned for the area. Around 1,500 people had come to the Laindon High Road School to hear for themselves what was going on. The school hall, several classrooms and an area outside had to be used to accommodate all the visitors. In his book *Brink of Despair*, George Ross gives an eyewitness account of this meeting. He describes how the Chairman of Billericay Council, George French, opened the meeting and was immediately met by a wave of hostility:

> This impact of protest was directed at him and his
> Council who had been instrumental in favouring
> the building of the New Town. The general uproar
> continued for several minutes. Everyone in the school's
> assembly hall seemed to be in protest. Men and women
> alike rose to their feet in anger at his presence.[2]

When Lewis Silkin got a chance to speak, his words did little to allay people's fears. Indeed he probably heightened them by announcing that those residents who owned the freehold to their property, the vast majority of the plotlanders who had bought their little plots of land, would not be able to keep it: 'Freeholds should be in the hands of the community and any transfer of land should be leasehold only.'[3]

For the residents who had probably previously rented rooms or houses in London (just like their parents and grandparents before them) and might therefore have been the first in their family to own their own piece of land, this edict from above constituted an intolerable outrage.

The Residents' Protection Association

Within weeks Resident Protection Associations had been formed in Laindon, Vange, Basildon, Pitsea and Dunton. George Ross was involved in the Laindon branch as his family owned land in New Century Road. When an Executive Committee was formed to co-ordinate the work of all branches he held the roles of secretary for five years and chairman for twenty.

The Association's first battle was the battle to retain the freeholds, and they tried myriad methods of protest. For example, leaflets with titles such as 'The Stupidity of the New Town' were produced and handed out in the area. Letters of complaint were written to the Minister. The Association also organised a banner-waving, slogan-chanting march to Downing Street to hand in a 3,000-signature petition, and in 1951 a letter was sent to Winston Churchill, who replied giving his support for their position. In the same year they even wrote a letter explaining the residents' plight to the Secretary of the United Nations. However, as this was regarded as 'a question of domestic jurisdiction' the UN could make no comment on the situation.[4] A change of Minister eventually brought an assurance that not all freehold rights would automatically be seized.

The Establishment of Basildon Development Corporation

It was against this backdrop of local unrest that BDC came into being on 3 February 1949 and its eight members, with Sir Lancelot Keay as Chairman, had the job of overseeing the task of building the new town and incorporating the existing population. Until it gained a local base, the Corporation had to work out of two rooms in London provided by the Ministry of Town and Country Planning. The lack of space and the distance from Basildon hampered its early work. It may also have contributed to a general feeling that the Corporation was remote from local people. One of the first appointments was the Chief Architect and Planner, Noel Tweddell, who was immediately tasked with preparing the Master Plan for the 7,834 acres of land which fell within the designated area.

In October 1949 the Corporation managed to secure a local base at Gifford House in Basildon, which was to remain its headquarters throughout its life. The Corporation took on more staff and began carrying out the various surveys required by the Chief Architect for the creation of the Master Plan. It took over six months to complete surveys of the area, which covered topography, geology, land use, age and condition of property (see chapter 2), farm units, sites of buildings of historical interest, roads, sewerage, gas, electricity, water and bus routes.

From the outset the Corporation knew it had a difficult job on its hands. The existing population of around 25,000 was larger than any its fellow new towns had to accommodate. In the first of its annual reports to the Minister of Town and Country, the Corporation was at pains to point out that it faced a planning problem of 'peculiar difficulty'. Describing the views of the existing population, the report went on to say:

> Many of the existing inhabitants are old age pensioners and many again eke out their livelihood by cultivating small holdings. There is a widespread apprehension among such people that the development of the new town will ultimately involve the loss of their freeholds; some welcome the amenities and improved standards of living that the new town may be expected to provide but fear that they might not be able to afford them. The decision to develop a new town of Basildon is therefore viewed with mixed feelings by any of those who live here.

In addition, the effect of various enactments governing the compensation to be paid by the Corporation for vacant possession inevitably restricts

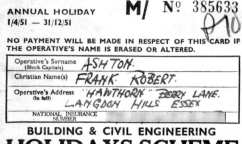

Typical holiday stamp cards for a local building worker from the 'New Town'.

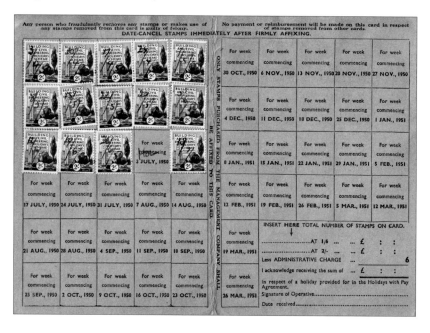

the sale of houses within the designated area, and in certain cases causes genuine hardship, thus hindering the Corporation's efforts to win the confidence and co-operation of the inhabitants.[5]

Interim Development

One of the first issues the Corporation had to tackle was how to control development in the area during the lengthy period before the Master Plan was finalised. After all, it had enough existing properties to worry about. In fact, it took until November 1950 before the Draft Plan was published to the sceptical locals. At its second meeting the Corporation confirmed that it wished to prevent, as far as possible, all development within the designated area while the plan was being created. It agreed that no development would be permitted in the 'open' areas' and that 'applications for infilling in already substantially built-up parts of the area would be dealt with on their merits'.[6] These latter areas were known as 'retention areas' where the Corporation proposed that the existing layout should be retained.

The Corporation was also concerned that house owners might start making substantial extensions to their properties, which could increase the amount of compensation payable in future. To prevent this, the Corporation stipulated that 'if extensions to properties are permitted it would be a condition of approval that no additional compensation payable for the extension in the event of compulsory purchase'.[7]

In July 1949 the Corporation decided that although no major works would be permitted in the clearance areas, it would permit minor works (up to £100 in value) but only when it was 'unlikely that the property will be required for 10 years or more'.[8] In reality, many people would undertake extensions or improvements to their property without seeking formal approval.

Even within a few months of setting this latest policy, the Chief Architect had to report to the Corporation's Board that in some cases the policy 'caused considerable hardship' and that such a policy would 'probably in particular cases, not be upheld by the Minister on appeal'. He therefore proposed that the Corporation should acquire suitable land 'to offer alternative building sites to people in clearance areas'.[9] This was adopted as policy in 1950.

The Master Plan

A draft of the Master Plan was revealed to the public in the autumn of 1950. It was published in the local press and put on display at an exhibition prepared by the Chief Architect's Department. The Corporation invited opinions, but the plan included the following plea: 'Please do not be wholly destructive, as this achieves nothing.'[10]

The following account of the public's reaction to the exhibition at Langdon Hills, which opened on Monday 27 November, was made to Basildon Development Corporation's monthly board meeting on 8 December 1950.

> Attendance has been good from the start. A large number of queries have been asked, a considerable proportion of which are outside the orbit of the Corporation, e.g. rights of compensation and claims for the loss of development rights. Visitors appeared mainly interested in what was to happen to their own particular property, but intelligent interest was also shown in the project as a whole. The impression has been gained by officials in attendance that on the whole the Plan has not been ill-received, although in one or two cases officials were subjected to insulting remarks by hostile visitors. It has also been noted that a certain number of people appear to be present by roster throughout the hours of opening, not to satisfy their own curiosity but to tackle other visitors, presumably with the intention of intensifying anti-New Town propaganda.[11]

A final plan for a population of 80,000 was sent to the Minister for approval in February 1951.

While going through the archives I came across a large coloured copy of the Master Plan. Until then I had only seen small black and white versions that appeared in the press. I wondered if this had been how the plan had been displayed to the public. The plan was huge, with a scale of six inches to a mile. Using this scale it was possible to see the individual plots in the existing plotland lanes, with the new town superimposed on top of it. The area was divided into colour-coded sections to denote what was intended

View of Hill Top Rise from 'Rose Villa' looking north towards railway, early 1950s.

Similar view as the new High View Avenue was built in 1990. Photo taken roughly at Arcadian Gardens looking towards Hill Top Rise. Today this is the section of road between the new Denehurst Gardens and Egerton Drive.

for that section: brown for residential; purple for industrial; blue for shops and businesses; red for administrative, educational, religious or cultural; various shades of green to denote open spaces or games areas; green and white stripes for allotments.

I felt a surprising intensity of emotion at seeing plots earmarked for development that once belonged to plotlanders I had recently met. A strange echo of dismay swept over me when I saw that one side of Helmore Crescent in Laindon, where Sheila Mountfort's family owned plots, was in a brown 'residential' zone. I knew that they had been compulsorily purchased in the 1970s. Indeed I remember wandering around the area as a child when the housing development commenced. Seeing the plots within the clearance area shouldn't have been a revelation to me. The plan had come to fruition and their destruction was all in the past. Nevertheless, this cold official announcement of their fate made me wonder what on earth it must have felt like when the plan was an indication of the future, not a record of the past.

Land Acquisition

Once the Master Plan had finally been approved the Corporation set about its task in earnest. It had already begun acquiring land, but had been careful not to build up too large a land bank. On the whole it only sought to purchase land that would be needed for development in the next couple of years. Nevertheless there are plenty of examples in the Corporation's minutes of what they called 'opportunistic purchases'. Here are just a few from the areas covered in this book:

- September 1951 – 'Myrtle' in Second Avenue Dunton. Purchased from Thurrock Urban District Council for £400 plus legal costs of £58 2s. 6d.[12]
- November 1951– 'Virginia' in Fourth Avenue. Purchased from Thurrock Urban District Council for £350 plus costs.[13]
- May and September 1955 – two parcels of scrubland in Hillcrest Avenue, one 0.33 acres and the other 0.138 acres.[14]

The task of purchasing land was huge. The problem was not that the Corporation faced many objections in the early years. Indeed, it carefully sought to develop open areas first so it wouldn't have to tackle the difficulty of rehousing too many people. The major problem was the fact that the land was owned by so many people. This made it a time-consuming and costly process. In its second annual report to the Minister in March 1951 the Corporation noted that:

> Fragmentation of land into numerous small plots, many of unknown ownership and others carrying nothing more than 'squatters' rights', makes the acquisition of land a long and laborious process, besides increasing materially the costs of acquisition. As an example, the purchase of some 46 acres of land ... will involve no less than 115 separate acquisitions: 53 of the plots to be acquired have no known owners, so far as can be ascertained at present.[15]

Harry Bacon was Head of the Planning and Transportation Department when BDC transferred its responsibility to the Commission for New Towns in 1986. When interviewed for this book he recalled that during its lifetime the Corporation 'had purchased 6,606 acres of land including 6,919 properties and involving some

Joe Bruce's bungalow in Brentford Avenue off Markhams Chase, Laindon, in 1950s. Typical of the properties that were compulsorily purchased.

14,000 ownerships. About 28% of the vacant land acquired was of unknown ownership so that the Corporation had to use Compulsory Purchase Order procedures.'

Compulsory Purchases and Voluntary Sales

The Corporation's original policy was to acquire land by agreement in the first instance and only use compulsory powers if necessary. However, from a very early stage it came under pressure from the Minister to accelerate the house-building programme (even before the Master Plan had been approved). At its monthly meeting in July 1950 the General Manager reported that the Corporation's policy of land acquisition was the main stumbling block when it came to meeting the Minister's wishes and that:

> if the Minister's strongly expressed wishes are to be met,
> the present policy of acquisition by agreement will have
> to be abandoned, although the political repercussions of
> such a step may need to be carefully considered.[16]

Whenever BDC wished to issue a Compulsory Purchase Order it had to get agreement from the Minister first. It was paradoxically common for a Minister to refuse the request, and sometimes the Corporation had to conduct protracted negotiations with him. Once a Compulsory Purchase Order was issued to a plot holder, he or she had the right of appeal to the Minister in writing within 28 days. However, if the appeal was refused then the Compulsory Purchase Order would come into force.

In the early years, the Corporation did not have to issue many Compulsory Purchase Orders. In its 1952 report to the Minister it noted that: 'It is with some satisfaction to report that, with only one exception, it has been possible to acquire lands [254 acres] by agreement with the owners.'[17] Two years later in the 1954 report it was noted that:

> On the whole, the number of objections to acquisition
> remains gratifyingly small, while even more gratifying
> is the ever increasing number of orders to sell to the
> Corporation. Not all these can at the moment be
> accepted, but the offers themselves are evidence that
> the value of good development is gradually being
> appreciated.[18]

By March 1955 the Corporation had reached the milestone of having built 2,000 houses, and the number of people approaching it to sell their land was growing rapidly. In March 1955 the Corporation reported that:

> As the Corporation's detailed proposals for the various
> areas become better known, a continually increasing

number of offers is being received … such offers during
the year just ended amounted to 545, and again showed
a considerable increase compared with the previous
year when there were no more than 177. Local owners
are becoming increasingly conscious of Section 6 (4) of
the New Towns Act which will come into operation in
Basildon in Jan. 1956, and it may be expected that the
number of offers both before and after that date will
continue to increase.[19]

Section 6 (4) gave owners the right to serve notice on the
Corporation to buy their plot. Within the first 12 weeks of this new
section of the Act coming into operation,
136 notices to purchase under this section
were served upon the Corporation.[20]
Harry Bacon told me:

> These were known as 'blight
> notices' – compulsory purchase
> in reverse! So many owners took
> advantage of this provision that the
> Corporation accumulated a large
> debt. Any money the Corporation
> needed – other than subsidies for
> housing – had to be borrowed from
> the Treasury and paid back over 60
> years at the current market rate of
> interest. The Treasury were none
> too pleased either.

Deanna at the end of
Bridge Avenue, 1976.
Roof of farmhouse
on caravan site in
background.

Same view in 1990.
Mandeville Way
being built over the
railway line.

By 1959 the Corporation seemed to be sweeping all before it. It demolished 219 substandard dwellings in that year, bringing the total to 1,226 plots.[21] However, the Corporation signalled that it was moving into a new phase of development, and its attention was turning towards Pitsea, Laindon, Vange and Langdon Hills. It felt these areas would bring 'the most difficult tasks of redevelopment … where many existing properties will be retained and the lines of many roads followed … leading to what is hoped will be the final task of returning to agricultural use certain sparsely developed areas outside the urban fence'.[22]

In the late 1960s the Corporation began to face more resistance. There were fierce battles when they tried to develop the Aquatels Recreation Centre on Pipps Hill Close in 1971, and they met with much opposition when they published the South West Area Plan, which encompassed Laindon, Langdon Hills and Dunton. We shall return to this topic in the next chapters.

Valuations and Compensation

Pages of statistics on the number of properties bought and demolished can easily mask the human face of the story. Staff had to bear in mind that every plot represented someone's home. Harry Bacon explained: 'It was for the Corporation planners to substantiate the case for acquisition but the Estates Officers were then responsible for negotiations with the owners.' For example, when the Corporation was first building the Barstable Estate in November 1952 the Chief Estates Officer went to see the owners. Hearing more about their circumstances he expressed his concerns over the disruption that would be caused to two of the elderly residents should they be forced to move. His report also raises an interesting issue regarding compensation:

a) I was favourably impressed by the general desire to co-operate, after the proposed development had been explained. Generally speaking, willingness to sell depended upon price. This is understandable, yet I found no evidence of inflated ideas of value.

b) However co-operative the owners were initially, my staff reports indicate that some subsequent negotiations conducted by District Valuer's staff has resulted in the 'evaporation' of the willingness to sell![23]

The Corporation had no influence over the amount offered to individual plot owners. Valuations were carried out by the District Valuer. Many of the bitter local disputes were due to the valuation given to the property. One of the Chairs of the Residents' Protection Association, Mr Parry, campaigned hard against perceived injustices in the value of land, noting differences between different areas.

In particular, where the property was timber and judged to be substandard by the District Valuer, less compensation was payable. This was of no help to the owners who simply could not afford to live elsewhere. George Ross described how the Residents' Protection Association was often able to assist owners in their negotiations with the District Valuer and at the Land Tribunal if the owner decided to take the case forward. This could be a risky strategy because if they lost the case they would then be liable for any costs.[24]

In some cases plot owners were able to maximise their compensation by dividing up a large plot and selling it in two transactions. George Ross explained that his parents did this with their plot, 'Gracelyn' in New Century Road, which is now the site of Merrylands School. Sheila Mountfort says that her parents and grandfather were able to do the same when they sold their plots 'Tetherdown' and 'Davos' in Helmore Crescent in the 1970s. These plots were very long and had frontages on both Helmore Crescent and Woodlands Road.

Anger about compensation still rankles after all these years. Phylis Frasi described how her mother was eventually forced to leave 'Ruby' in Berry Drive in the early 1980s. She said her mother didn't get much for the timber rendered property because the land was earmarked for return to agricultural use. However, a housing estate was later built on the area.

Nina Humphrey also describes bitterly how she feels her parents lost out on compensation when their bungalow and acre of land in Alexandra Drive was compulsorily purchased in 1975. They, too, were assured that the land was not going to be used for development, but subsequently dozens of houses and maisonettes were built there. Her parents had also spent over 20 years tending three acres of neighbouring land that had been abandoned by its former owners (the Coopers), but were unable to claim 'squatters' rights'. Nina explains:

> During the early sixties, somebody pointed out to my parents that if you have tended a piece of waste ground for a number of years, you can legally claim it for yourself and advised them to instruct a solicitor. The solicitor informed them that firstly the land must be insured and he would make the arrangements. However, after a few weeks he returned saying that he was unable to find any Insurance Company willing to take on the job, due to the land being so close to Basildon New Town. My parents were very disappointed and unfortunately decided not to pursue their claim any further.

'Ruby' in Berry Drive, 1950s.

During the heartbreaking compulsory purchase from 1973 to 1975 my parents started looking for a new home to buy with the compensation they were to be offered. They instructed the same solicitor to handle their case, who negotiated with the Corporation on their behalf. Originally they were offered a substantial amount of compensation, certainly enough to buy another bungalow and piece of land elsewhere in Essex. The solicitor advised them not to accept the offer immediately as he thought he could push the amount up a little higher. That turned out to be the wrong advice, because just two weeks after receiving the original offer from the Corporation, my parents received notification that the offer had been halved, the explanation being that the value of land had dropped and that poor drainage on their plot made the land unsuitable for building. This further dreadful disappointment caused them to lower their sights but they eventually found a very nice suitable bungalow in Great Burstead. In the years following their move, builders did exactly what the Corporation said couldn't be done. They built new houses where 'Spion Kop' and its piece of land had been.

What Type of Housing?

Nina's parents decided against moving into a new Corporation home, but many plotlanders did move onto one of the new estates. Those who did might lose their large plot of land, but would gain a property with modern amenities. It was initially the job of the Chief Architect, Noel Tweddell, to decide what kind of housing would be built in Basildon, taking into account government research into housing for the post-war society. Bearing in mind that a large number of the new tenants would be coming from London, he consulted J. Austin, the Chief Housing Officer for East Ham Council.

In a candid letter dated 14 July 1950 he expressed his difficulties in designing houses 'for a population whose requirements I do not know through long experiences with them'. He asked for advice on the proportion of two-, three-, four- and five-bedroom houses, the ratio of flats to houses, and the ratio of gardens and allotments to dwellings. [25] In his reply of 20 July Mr Austin said, from personal experience, 95 per cent of people preferred houses to flats[26] – an interesting statistic given the amount of flat-building that went on in the London boroughs in the post-war period.

In deciding how many bedrooms each property should have, J. Austin conducted a survey of the building operatives who wanted to relocate to Basildon in the first wave of new tenants. This was a sensible measure because, as the Corporation noted in its first annual report: 'As with nearly all new towns the availability of building labour will largely govern the rate of building and civil engineering development.'[27] The survey showed that 288 workers wanted to relocate, including bricklayers, carpenters, decorators, plumbers, scaffolders, labourers and the like. The majority (159) requested two-bedroom houses, 67 requested one-bedroom houses and 52 requested three-bedroom houses.[28]

The next stage was to design the layout for the different types of houses. Miss J. Albery was the architect in charge of the housing accommodation. In a 1951 Report on Household Structure and Housing Needs the Corporation had to consider what its general housing stock should look like, taking into account the costs of various materials used in the designs.

Eventually a series of designs were created and these had to be approved by the Corporation members. Many of the early houses appeared to be traditional in appearance and layout, but by the time some of the estates were being built in Laindon in the 1960s and 1970s, the designs had become more innovative. As the late Colin Ward wrote in 1974: 'The intentional haphazard design pays a gentle compliment to Shacksville.'[29]

The Corporation *versus* the Local Council

Of course, the Corporation wasn't the only body interested in building properties in the area. Some private developers were allowed to build small estates, and the local council was also permitted some limited development. However, it became apparent that competing demands for building land began to create tension between the Corporation and the local council. Billericay Council had been instrumental in getting the New Town designated in its area, but looking through the archives there is evidence of a growing frustration as its plans for building its own stock of council housing were stymied in some areas. For example, the council houses that were finally built in Bourne Avenue and Bourne Close, which were adjacent to 'Spion Kop', took almost a decade to build after protracted negotiations with the Corporation.

Difficulties over territorial rights seemed to reach a head in April 1964 when Charles Boniface, the General Manager of the Corporation, wrote a stiff letter to Alma Hatt, Clerk of the Basildon Urban District Council (as it was called after 1954). Mr Boniface reiterated that there was no point in the council seeking to acquire land in areas where the Corporation had not accepted its proposals. It appeared that the council had been caught red-handed trying to make purchases of land around Pitsea within the boundaries of the designated area, thereby bringing it in competition with the Corporation. Mr Boniface wrote:

Nina Humphrey at 'Spion Kop'. New housing in Bourne Close reached their garden in mid-1960s. It enabled them to build a path to avoid the unmade muddy roads.

I am sure you will agree that this discloses an undesirable state of affairs and one that should not be allowed to continue. I shall be glad if you would therefore affirm that your Council will confine its acquisition programme to those areas which it has been agreed in principle should be developed by you.[30]

However, former Planning Office staff have told me that this 'tiff' quickly blew over and on the whole relations between the councillors and Corporation officers were very good. Indeed, Alma Hatt was held in high regard by Corporation staff.

A Home of Your Own

Looking through the records it is clear that the Corporation had to adapt to changing national policy as Labour and Conservative governments pushed their different approaches in relation to landownership. There was a big difference between the insistence of the Labour Minister Lewis Silkin on replacing all freeholds with leaseholds and the Thatcherite policies which pushed for the disposal of public housing in favour of freeholds.

There were many subtle shifts in between. I smiled ironically when I came across the following document. In June 1973, a period when many plotlanders, including some I have met personally, were losing their freehold properties in the west of Laindon, the Corporation reached another milestone. A family in a road called Brendon in the Laindon 5 Housing Area became the 5,000th purchasers of a Corporation home. The Conservative Minister for Housing and Construction, Paul Channon, sent the following congratulatory letter to the family:

The Government believe that it is most important that those who wish to own their own homes should be able to do so. Yours is the 5,000th house which Basildon Development Corporation have sold to one of their tenants. I am sure you will agree that the Corporation have thus made an important contribution to achieving this aim.[31]

I couldn't help wondering who had been displaced from the land on which the house in Brendon was built, thus enabling another family to own their own home. Ironically, Brendon itself disappeared from the map in the mid-1990s when the flats and maisonettes were demolished and replaced with the Armada Estate.[32] This pattern has been repeated on several of the estates built in the 1960s around Laindon. Those new estates, heralds of the modern world, didn't actually last as long as many of the little wooden shacks they replaced.

Chapter 15

The Bulldozers Arrive

Much of Laindon town was redeveloped with new housing estates in the 1960s and the character of the town began to change dramatically. This fact was not lost on the local council and in its Official Guide to Basildon Urban District of 1968 it noted: 'The Corporation are continuing the acquisition of land and properties within the designated area and a major attack on the redevelopment areas of Laindon and Vange has begun … '[1] With reassuring language like that being used in the council's official guide, local residents must have envisaged panzer divisions heading over the horizon at any moment. No doubt redundant Anderson shelters were hastily being cleared out, and old gas masks dragged from the back of cupboards and sheds.

The 'major attack' was simply the Corporation executing its revised Master Plan. In November 1964 the Minister for Housing and Local Government instructed the Corporation to explore the possibility of expansion at Basildon, as suggested in the government's 1964 South East Study. Harry Bacon, then the Senior Planner in the Department of Architecture and Planning, was tasked with assessing the maximum population that could be accommodated and then preparing a new plan. Harry recalled that the government had a figure of 200,000 in mind but after comprehensive research to evaluate the physical, social and economic factors, the Corporation concluded that it would be possible to increase the target population from 106,000 to only 140,000, to which the government reluctantly agreed.

Harry told me why a new Master Plan was necessary:

> There had been fundamental social and economic changes in the country since the first Master Plan was agreed in 1951 and it was recognised that a complete revision of the Master Plan and underlying policies was essential. Of particular significance for plotland owners in the South West Area (and elsewhere) was the formal abandonment of the 1951 policy of returning surplus land to agriculture and smallholdings, which was not seen to be economic. In order to maximise the population increase, all suitable land capable of drainage by gravitation was included within the 'urban fence'. Thus some plotlands

were recognised as having potential for development in future years while others came within recreational or wildlife conservation areas. Therefore there was a change for some in the way compensation was assessed.

The revised Master Plan was publicised in September 1966 with a large exhibition in the Town Centre and smaller displays throughout the town. Numerous objections were received. Alan Radford, the Estates Officer, and I visited residents by appointment in their homes to explain how the proposals would affect their property either directly or indirectly. In consequence, the fears of many people were allayed and objections withdrawn.

Nevertheless, it was not possible to satisfy everyone and the remaining objectors had an opportunity to state their views at a public inquiry in February 1967. Among the objectors were the Essex and District Councils, the Residents' Protection Association, Roland Partridge, who, like his father before him, farmed very successfully at Dry Street Farm for many years, and naturalist Stan Hollands who was Chair of Basildon Natural History Society.

The Minister decided that the plan should be amended, and subsequently two neighbourhoods, Hawkesbury (Dry Street Farm) and Kingston Ridge, north of Dry Street, were excluded. These amendments were welcomed by residents, and Harry was also pleased that this area of farmland and beautiful countryside had been saved from development. He had only included them in the plan in order to meet the Minister's original population target. The work then started on a new plan for the South West Area.

The early 1970s were not an easy period for the Corporation for a variety of reasons. In April 1973 it considered a report from the General Manager about the crisis in house building. The national building strike in the late summer of 1972 had delayed the completion of houses and the Corporation was way behind schedule. According to Mr Boniface the first three months of 1973 had been 'the most serious he remembered in the history of the Corporation'.[2]

Clearly the Corporation was coming under pressure from a number of directions, as their reduced output of homes coincided with an increase in demand. There were over 1,500 on the waiting list and this was expected to rise to 2,200 within the year. However, the forecast for completed houses in the next year was only 507 and as well as demand from local people, the General Manager reported that the Corporation 'were constantly being reminded of their duty to London … '[3]

The South West Area Plan was revised again and still met with fierce opposition. Public inquiries were held in November 1974 and October 1975, but it was not just the local residents who were

Helmore Crescent in 1969, looking towards Laindon.

Now called Durham Road, the same view taken in 2009.

objecting. Thurrock Council, which had once included the Dunton Hills Estate within its boundary, had major concerns that new housing would spoil the views of Langdon and Dunton Hills that could be seen by its residents from miles away.[4]

The various drafts of the plan had to undergo major revisions to meet the principal objections, including the exclusion of a whole neighbourhood of 1,200 people which had been planned for Dunton, and the establishment of a Dunton Hills development set back from the brow of the hills so it would not be seen from afar. Had these victories not been won by the objectors, the area would look very different today.

Despite uncertainty about the approval of its South West Area Plan the Corporation had to continue with everyday business, including buying land in the area in which it was planning to build, such as the Great Berry area. In June 1974 the Corporation agreed to issue a Compulsory Purchase Order for 19.1 acres of land in the Great Berry Housing Area 2, and by this time the Corporation already owned most of this area.[5] It also started on important infrastructure projects such as the extension to Durham Road (Road 31) which would run parallel with the railway and become the main spine for the new Laindon West (or Laindon 8) estates.

In October 1974 the Corporation approved Compulsory Purchase Orders in readiness for the Laindon 8 phase of development which was due to commence in 1976.[6] In March 1975 the Corporation reported that:

> During the year the main planning activity has been concerned with the South West Area Plan. This covers 1,582 acres or more than 20 per cent of the designated area. Whenever there has been a new master plan for the town it is here that there is most objection to the Corporation's proposals; and now that there has been some housing started, there is a realisation amongst the residents that it may not be long before the Corporation's proposals for the area will take effect on the ground.[7]

The planning process for the South West Area lasted for around nine years, over three times longer than it took to create and get approval for the original Master Plan for the whole of Basildon. It was not until July 1976 that the Secretary of State for the Environment finally agreed the plan.

A Weekender's View of the Encroaching Development

So what did all these machinations about planning and the gradual spread of new housing feel like to an average weekender? Below, I have chosen a few extracts from my mum's diaries from the 1970s and 1980s to show how the changes were perceived by a non-permanent

Glad and Deanna
walking along High
Bank Drive in the
mid-1970s.

resident as new estates were being lifted from the pages of plans and
beginning to take form on the ground. The extracts also mention
what was happening to some of the remaining plots in the area and
describe the final days of our own plot, 'Halliford'.

When Mum talks about walking round to see the building
work, I remember that most of the time we ended up wandering
around the Durham Road and Helmore Crescent area, drawn by a
strange compulsion to watch the ocean of concrete creep nearer and
nearer. These would have been the areas referred to as Road 31 (the
Durham Road Extension) and the Laindon 8 housing area. The final
western section of this area was virtually complete by March 1980.

Not being permanent residents or locals, we usually didn't have
a clue about the precise details of what was going on, so snatches of
information had to be gleaned from fellow weekenders, and from
the few permanent residents in the area.

These diary extracts also show the difficulties caused to
plotlanders as the Corporation started preparing the services that
would eventually be needed for the new housing. The arrival of a
mysterious concrete bunker near the entrance to Bridge Avenue
around 1974 heralded that something was afoot. We called it the
pumping station. It still lurks in the undergrowth off Hawthorn Path
today. At a similar point the old oak trees along the edge of Berry
Drive were uprooted, and the lane was churned up for the laying
of sewerage pipes. All this disruption meant that much of our time
seemed to be spent repairing the roads or worrying about the state of
them. My dad, Jack Darwin, had an old three-wheel Reliant, which
meant that it was even more problematic to get the car round if the
road was churned up.

'San Souci' in late 1960s. Left to right: Lil Bradley from 'Erma', Joe Hopgood, Deanna and Jack Darwin, Florrie Hopgood.

The very first diary entry talks about mending ruts in Berry Drive, outside my Uncle Joe's former property, 'San Souci'. The Hopgoods had owned the plot since 1955 and had put a chalet, caravan and an old wooden caravan on the site. Earlier in the 1970s thieves had burnt the wooden caravan to extract the metal chassis for scrap iron.

So let's look at what my mum said in her diaries. Where references are made to fellow plotlanders I have added some explanatory notes in brackets.

Tues 28 May 1974 (half-term)

Done lots more to the road right as far as Joe's. Hard going but we're winning. Deanna and I collected charcoal from Joe's to help fill in.

Spoke to Glad about the redevelopment but don't think much will come of it. Going home tomorrow. [Glad was a permanent resident who lived in 'Mill Den' in Hill Top Rise.]

Thurs 30 May 1974

Finished the road. Had to wait until gas men came and repaired leak in Ricky's place [unused weekender's plot in Berry Drive]. Someone broke gas pipe. In the early evening went and got the car, and brought it round. Lovely road we've made. Hope no-one ruins it. Been hearing the nightingale in the evenings.

Thurs 11 July 1974

Had letter from Nell saying Laindon having sewers laid and hard to get by. That's all we want. Perming Doll's hair this evening so asked to use her phone to call Glad. Glad said all alright. We should be able to get down alright. [Doll was our neighbor in Dagenham. Nell was a weekender who owned the neighbouring 'Barbrook' in High Bank Drive.]

Weds 27 July 1975 [school holidays]

After going to Southend … Jack was going home [to Dagenham] to take unwanted luggage but got stopped before we got to the bridge by workmen as it wasn't safe. They agreed to let us pass. Went round there later and found three fellows and a car dismantling Joe's place so had to stop them. Came back and decided to paint a sign for Joe's place saying 'private property'. Bridge seems alright. [The railway bridge was at the end of Bridge Avenue.]

The workmen continued to work in the area. As a result of the digging in the previous year, Berry Drive had become very churned up and the heavy clay soil brought to the surface. This made it a quagmire when it rained.

Skippy & Judy guarding 'Mill Den', 1976.

Sun 14 Sept 1975

Left about 10 o/c in morning, then stuck in mud round Joe's. Terrible. Rain and cold. We worked like Trojans to get out. Lugging great girders – wonder we were not all ill after. Finally made it getting on for 3 o/c. All fell in mud. Then went out past 'Whynot'. Quite easy! What a time. All had hot baths when we got home.

Fri 16 April 1976 – Good Friday

Popped down as it was dry … Joe's place collapsed altogether. Then we saw our fence veranda had broken. I said get four uprights from Joe's. Finished up carrying piles of wood.

Sat 5 June 1976

Nell and Charlie down ['Barbrook']. Deanna and I

went and saw the new road they are making past the woodman's house.

The new road was Road 31, the Durham Road Extension. The 'woodman's house' was 'Wide View' in Helmore Crescent which was owned by Sheila Mountfort's great-uncle Mr Davison (see p.52).

Sat 24 July 1976

Rabbits bashing around in the night again. Making a heck of a noise. Deanna & I walked round to see how the houses are being built.

Sat 14 Aug 1976

Ern [from 'Maple Leaf'] came before dinner to say a van was at Joe's place. When Jack got there they had gone with the loo and the other remains. [I think Mum is referring to bits of buildings rather than the contents of the loo!]

Thurs 19 Aug 1976

After dinner went to Langdon Hills. Long walk came out at Jim's shop then went to Durham Road where they are building.

Jim's shop was situated at the top of Berry Lane and was formerly known as the Lungleys' Victory Stores – from where Peter did his delivery round.

3 Oct 1976

Deanna & I went and made a run-way into ditch to empty a lake-sized puddle near Bridge Avenue and mended road.

9 Oct 1976

Deanna & I went and made road again. Maddening as we slog to do it and everybody rides over it churning it up. Still we enjoyed doing it.

16 June 1977

Walked to top where horses are [in fields either side of Forest Glade]. Deanna and I walked to where they are building houses. Certainly moved. Jill [from 'The Cabin' in Hill Top Rise] came round for Deanna.

Tues 16 Aug 1977

Jack making front door panelling. All fitted and being painted. Looks better. Deanna made a little tent house and been playing for hours. I'm writing this in it. When we settled in for the night I was reading to her when a beautiful storm started. Then the rain! It was terrible. Heard on radio Elvis Presley died.

Sat 20 Aug 1977

Sunny day. Deanna & I went to the Links shopping centre in Laindon. Muddy getting to Worthing Road. Came home Durham Road and I got huge sheet of plastic so heavy I had to hide it in 'The Lair' and Jack and Deanna went back for it. Bit holey but should be alright.

Deanna feeding horses in the field next to Forest Glade, mid-1970s. Today the new Forest Glade is roughly on this site.

In case you are wondering why Mum seemed to have taken a random fancy to a huge sheet of plastic, I should explain that we needed something to stop the rain getting in our caravan. Mum also mentions the empty plot belonging to 'The Lair' at the very end of Helmore Crescent, and Sheila Mountfort remembers this as being 'a fairy-tale type of bungalow which was very pretty with leaded windows'. It had been built prior to 1939 by the same architect who designed her family's plot 'Tetherdown'. The owners sold up to the Corporation.

Sun 21 Aug 1977

Mad blokes on motor bikes tearing up and down near pumping station have made that a quagmire [on section of road between Bridge Avenue and Berry Drive]. Then the horses done the rest round Joe's way. If it's not one thing it's another.

Fri 26 Aug 1977

Deanna and I worked on the road again. Then later cut the over-hanging branches. When we looked to see how our work looked, horses and cars had been all over it. We were very cross.

Holiday Monday 29 Aug 1977

Glad having van taking bricks back and forward so I went to see the road. Getting churned up.

At some point between the summer of 1977 (which is the last time they get a mention) and the summer of 1978 Glad and Alf had sold up their plot 'Mill Den' in Hill Top Rise.

Dunton caravan site in 1963.

11 Aug 1978

Called in at caravan office and spoke to Mr Gray [he was the manager of Dunton Caravan Park]. He said Council will make a road from Durham Road. We might have to use it. [Normally we drove down Lower Dunton Road, through the Dunton Caravan Park and took the unmade road that ran alongside the railway and then turned over the railway bridge.]

Tues 15 Aug 1978

Nell ['Barbrook'], Arthur and Lil [from 'Mill Haven' in Hill Top Rise] down. Still talking about all our places being taken over. Yet we heard from road workers not going to touch our way. Wait and see.

Sat 26 Aug 1978

Deanna and I went to shop. Heard them pulling down 'Burr View'. Walked up there.

Mon 23 July 1979

Walked around the block. Quite nice so far. Horses moved right over probably letting grass grow. Admirals Glen all churned up by gas men. Don't know why. [This was our nickname for the junction of Berry Drive and Western Ave where Red Admiral butterflies were a regular sight in the oak trees.]

Fri 27 July 1979

Got paper at Camp Shop. Very hot out. Just lazed outside in the sun reading. About 7.30pm someone set fire to 'Happy Jack's' place. Gosh did it go up. Poor Deanna. She was petrified. Don't think she'll settle here now in case they do 'The Dutchess'. I think we would be in trouble then as the bushes would spread over this side. Firemen here quick. Lots of people around. Police here after. Deanna all nerves. [Both were abandoned plots in High Bank Drive.]

Sat 28 July 1979

Deanna & I went to the Links shopping centre. Police called in about the fire damage. Said he'll make a report about 'The Dutchess'. Maybe the Council will pull it down. Spent a lot of time clearing the trees that touch down the lane. Deanna a bit easier but I think it's spoilt the holiday for her. She wants the rain.

Sat 26 July 1980

Mrs Jeeves [permanent resident from 'Tekowaia' Hill Top Rise] said Bridge Avenue all got notices to quit over road going in. Even 'Ruby' and 'Why Not' [both in Berry Drive].

Sun 24 Aug 1980

Florrie & Joe arrived. Went round their place ['San Souci'] and Joe got his apples. After eating went for a walk as far as The Avenues, then round to Lil's place [derelict 'Erma' plot in High View Avenue]. Sun shining

Members of Deanna's family at 'Erma' in late 1960s.

had a lovely day. Joe loves it at Laindon. Wonder how long we will be able to keep all our shacks?

Sat 27 Sept 1980

Decided to have a lie-in. Headache. Could be paraffin affecting sinus. Went to Camp Shop asked about gate that is ready to go across our way. She said he [Mr Gray?] won't shut it till we have another way in or maybe let us buy a key.

Thurs 3 Sept 1981

Jack mixed a good green colour and painted the front. Looks good. Deanna going to whiten the fence. I did cooking and clearing, and scraping down the side.

Sun 6 Sept 1981

Jack finished painting the house. It looks lovely. Deanna done all the white fence and posts. Back to school next day.

It is clear from mum's diary that by 1981 our trips to Laindon were becoming less and less frequent. Our week at 'Halliford' at the end of the school holidays in 1981 proved to be the last time we would stay overnight. I find it ironic, and rather sad, that we spent the week painting the hut and sprucing everything up, and yet it was really the last hurrah for our little plot. It proved to be naive to hope that a coat of bright paint could keep the outside world at bay – it didn't.

Tues 6 April 1982

Heard from Jean ['The Cabin', Hill Top Rise]. Said Laindon compulsory orders were right but still don't believe it. They just sent us rates. Trouble brewing in the Falklands.

Jack and Deanna, having finished painting 'Halliford' in 1981.

Tues 27 July 1982

Went to Laindon. Couldn't get the car down our track so I waited while they [Jack & Deanna] went on. After I followed and the shock! Everything was all over the place. Every drawer and cupboard had been ransacked. 2 Calor Gas cylinders gone. All the tools, the Mobo horse and bike. Poor 'Vyn' turned over [our old car]. Then two people came through from Nell's (also ransacked). Told them we were waiting for police. They went. Then four boys went by on bikes and heard them say that someone's there so I reckon they were the ones. It was awful there. Deanna wanted to get away after her tears. When we left it looked nice again. One thing, they hadn't smashed everything.

Thurs 29 July 1982

Went to Laindon. Deanna a nervous wreck. Still all was well. Jack scythed front. We packed some stuff and brought it home. We'll wait on Council's reply to find out what to do. Jack doesn't want to get rid of it now. Said it doesn't take him long to cut grass.

Mon 2 Aug 1982

Jack & I went to Laindon. Turned very hot. He cut more grass in front. It looks as though we are there now.

By 1983 we had decided not to keep our plot. I think we all found it hard to reconcile the happy carefree memories of summers spent at 'Halliford' with the unsafe atmosphere that we experienced when we visited the previous summer. I know I certainly didn't want the image of break-ins to taint my memories of our plot. However, it was very hard for Dad to give up on the place that had been a dream to him. Reading Mum's diary I suddenly remembered that it was the arrival of the rates bill in 1983 that finally made him take the decision to sell. We had very little money so Dad reluctantly accepted that we simply couldn't afford to pay out rates on somewhere that we might only visit to repair damage caused by vandals.

Sun 3 April 1983

Deanna typed a letter to Basildon Council to see what they'll offer for our place.

Fri 29 April 1983

Went to Laindon. What a shock and sight! All smashed up. Just a write-off. Sad to think of how it was and now all gone. Takes a bit to sink in. Jim's shop gone now. No horses there also [in fields along Forest Glade]. What a thing to happen. Good job Deanna didn't see it.

Thurs 5 May 1983

Heard from Basildon. Said going to ask Valuer to see if he can make an offer.

6 Oct 1983

Heard from solicitor. £2,800. That's good.

2 Dec 1983

Florrie and Joe [San Souci] came dinner time. Told them about getting Laindon money (it came today).

And that was that. Over 30 years of plot ownership ended with the arrival of a cheque. It seemed so anti-climactic when I found this diary entry. What was I expecting to find? A Shakespearean soliloquy beginning: 'Alas poor "Halliford", I knew it well'? I guess that by the time we got the cheque it was just a matter of finishing the transaction, and not a time for sentimental thoughts.

Over the next few years we still made occasional trips to see what was happening in the area. We were amazed by the speed at which Nature had reclaimed the abandoned plots and lanes. It was becoming a struggle to walk down High Bank Drive, and yet it had only been a couple of years since we had been able to drive along it. I made the odd trip down with my husband in the late 1980s and 1990s, but the last time I made the trip with my parents was a couple of days before I left home for university in 1985: the end of one era and the start of another.

Deanna outside the front of 'Halliford', 1975

Chapter 16

The 1980s - Final Days

In early 1984, just a couple of months after we had sold our plot, Mark McManus discovered the Dunton plotlands. Immediately captivated by the area he spoke to some of the remaining residents and managed to photograph the final days of many of the plots. I am so grateful that he did, because he is now able to offer us a poignant vision of the end of an era. Here is his story:

'A scrubland full of ghosts,
And memories of happier times.'

This is how I once described the Dunton plotlands to a friend, because I was an interloper rather than a plotlander. I arrived very late on the scene, in time to see this remarkable social movement come to a controversial and sometimes emotional end.

Since moving from East London to Langdon Hills at the age of 10, I had always been aware of the 'history' of the area. My new home adjoined the Nature Reserve which later became known as 'Mark's Hill', and strolling around those woods always invoked a sense of claustrophobic mystery. Older maps revealed that the paths through these woods once had names such as Gladstone Road, Albemarle Crescent, Nightingale Avenue.

I first encountered the Dunton plotlands in February 1984, while following the route of the Basildon Nature Trail. This trail began in Vange and snaked across the golf course and Langdon Hills, before terminating at the foot of Second Avenue.

My first visit, accidental as it was, captivated me immediately. It was a revelation of local history, a peripheral reminder of the foundations upon which Basildon New Town had been raised. The old neighbourhoods, transformed over years into rich meadows and dense scrub, had an essence which sent shivers down the spine. It was a scrubland full of ghosts and memories of happier times, a doomed vision of human endeavour, love and resourcefulness. The eerie, pervasive sensation of that first visit was that I had inadvertently stumbled across the passing of something important, a brief social movement that would never be repeated.

I spent hours on that day criss-crossing the grids of tracks that made up the Dunton plotlands, gazing at the few remaining bungalows and holiday homes, staring at the piles of rubble overgrown by bramble, inspecting the derelict shacks with their nameplates forlornly intact, consumed by a sense of regret and yearning. I wanted to transport myself back in time, wanted to see this area when the grass was short and the paint on the shacks was still fresh, not peeling from crumbling wood.

The greatest impression, the one that drew me back to Dunton weeks later with a camera, was the area based around Hill Top Rise, now mostly buried beneath new housing and Tesco's (see map, p.92). There was a tightly knit cluster of plots here that, quite clearly, had become derelict in the very recent past. I remember cursing myself for not having taken this personal voyage of discovery a year earlier, when this particular avenue and its environs would have looked much different. It was the *Marie Celeste* of the Dunton plotlands. Whereas the other plots – be they occupied or derelict – tended to be isolated, separated by stretches of hawthorn scrub or tangled overgrown gardens, the recently abandoned plots in and around Hill Top Rise were all neighbours. A small community had existed here, and had entirely vanished during the frustratingly irretrievable recent past.

Bulldozer tracks had left their scars across many of the plots, especially those in High View Avenue. They had cleared these plots so completely that it was impossible to trace the boundaries between them. Others were far more evocative: two of the buildings had been destroyed by fire, the grass on the lawn in front of the burned remains of 'The Cabin' was still short and the plot's chain-link fence remained intact (although the front gate had disappeared). Foliage had yet to venture across the ashes and charred timbers of 'Good View', and the name of that building remained forlornly emblazoned upon its two gate posts. I found this curiously upsetting. The name, two syllables, one to each wooden post, proudly announcing the existence of a building which lay in a huddle of scorched wood before me ... and a 'good view' of what?

Other plots in this cluster were easier to define. 'Rose Villa', in a very ruinous state, remained standing: a small

Hill Top Rise in the 1960s. Jack Darwin in the garden of 'Mill Haven'. Plots in High View Avenue in the background.

wooden building on its last legs, leaning precariously and (in a very human touch) with the tattered remnants of net curtains still fluttering through denuded windows. 'Halliford', with its frontage on High Bank Drive, could also be defined. The rear was gone, crushed by the bulldozers, and no evidence remained of the shack itself, but its front hedge stood proud, complete with a postbox for a building that no longer existed, while chicken wire defined the three remaining sides of this small rectangular plot. I strolled in the 'Halliford' plot and a pheasant took flight, only to crash into and struggle with the chicken wire before breaking free and squawking into the undergrowth. What better example of nature replacing human effort?

Other derelicts stood in the neighbouring avenues. In the otherwise completely overgrown High View Avenue stood a lonely hut named 'Roseview', its nameplate also announcing the name of its owner, a Mr Jeeves. To the rear of 'Good View', with a frontage on Arcadian Gardens, stood an abandoned bungalow, 'Joyce', and at the other end of that same avenue stood anonymous twin shacks. Their doors hung open and splintered, clothing and

colouring books scattered and shredded. On one leaf I
found a child's poignant scrawl: 'This book belongs to
Jane Hibell.' Just around the corner in Glenwood Gardens
stood the 'White House', the estate's only remaining two-
storey building, now denuded and over-grown.

I noticed, during my perambulations, that the surviving
derelict buildings tended to cluster close to plots that
were still occupied – a fact which presumably acted
as a deterrent to vandals. There were signs of recent
abandonment and destruction throughout Dunton Hills:
barely a single avenue did not bear the traces of recent loss.

I returned two months later, armed with a camera,
to find that 'Rose Villa' had finally collapsed, 'Joyce'
had been demolished, one of the twin huts in Arcadian
Gardens had burned down and the upper storey of 'White
House' had also succumbed to flames. As well as this, the
Compulsory Purchase Orders had arrived. These notices,
dreaded by plotlanders since the New Town Act of 1949,
were attached to stakes and driven into the ground in front
of every private plot. They listed all the plots, gave the
buildings' names where they were known, and announced
the intention of the Corporation to possess all of the land
either for building or for the creation of a new country
park. These notices were followed, a few months later, by
a new wave of notices called General Vesting Declarations.

These notices, along with the use of Electoral
Registers held at Basildon Library, allowed me to identify

'Colin' in Crest
Avenue, 1984.

'Chook-a-berry' in Western Avenue, 1984.

many of the plots which otherwise would have remained nameless, and the photographs I took were among the last ever taken of the remaining buildings – the second hut in Arcadian Gardens was destroyed very shortly after I took its picture.

'Colin', Crest Avenue: The main building had burned down in September 1983 on the same night as 'Roseville' in Beech Hall Gardens. The former was owned by Ronald Cakebread of Canning Town, the latter by his relative, Edwin Howson. I paid Mr Cakebread a visit the year after this picture was taken, to see if he could add to my gradual enlightenment, and received tea and cake from his lovely wife! 'Colin' stood in an area clustered with derelicts: Crest Avenue itself contained two decrepit buildings to the east of 'Colin': a more recently abandoned shack at the corner of Crest Avenue and Beech Hall Gardens; and the remains of a blue caravan called 'Lakeside' which, according to Mr Cakebread, had been occupied by a gentleman called Sandy. A large pond filled much of this plot. The pond predated the rise of the neighbourhood and still exists today.

I came across some unnamed shacks in Arcadian Gardens. One of two huts on a single plot, its twin had burned down and, forlorn and violated, it was soon to follow. Arcadian Gardens had recently lost the buildings 'Joyce' and 'Fair Oak', and after this little shack was predictably destroyed the sole survivor would be a small pebble-dashed derelict called 'Florem' which, surprisingly, lasted until the bulldozers finally came.

'Chook-a-berry', Western Avenue: two caravans, side by side, which were occupied by the Blatch Family until they moved in November 1984. They owned two excitable Shetland sheepdogs who would start up a din if you dared walk past their territory! Dogs were a common feature of the Dunton Plotlands; of the remaining occupied plots, only 'Thorngrove' in First Avenue lacked a resident canine. As well as for companionship, dogs were an extra form of security for people living in such isolated situations.

'Grangewood', Beech Hall Gardens: as I walked past this cosy little bungalow at the junction of Highland

Gardens I noticed one of its occupants pottering about the front garden, and to my surprise I recognised her! I immediately asked, 'Mrs Haybell, do you remember me?'

She knew my face but could not recall my name. Mary Haybell had, until her recent retirement, been a teacher at the Lincewood Primary School which I had attended. She lived here, in the plotlands, with her husband, William, and two St Bernard dogs. We talked about the compulsory purchase notices which were then infesting the neighbourhood, and Mrs Haybell quietly claimed, 'I've been here too long … they'll never get me out.'

This hope was to prove false. Only a few weeks after their closest neighbours at 'Chook-a-berry' departed, the Haybells too packed their bags and left at the end of 1984. They did not move far; their new address was a few minutes' walk away in a road off Berry Lane. 'Grangewood', after suffering much at the hands of vandals, was finally demolished the following year.

'Grangewood' in Beech Hall Gardens. 1984.

'Rosemary' was the last derelict shack in Highland Gardens; its survival may have been due to the fact that the Haybells at 'Grangewood' lived only a stone's throw away. It was a small building, no larger than a typical garden shed, so my initial assumption was that it had been a holiday home. I was surprised to discover, upon reading the Electoral Registers, that a family called Wallace had claimed it as a residence in 1964. When I found and photographed 'Rosemary', it had a marked list; I expected it to fall down at any time. However, despite its neglect and its frail condition, 'Rosemary' managed to brave the elements for over a year before finally slumping into a defeated heap of timber in the spring of 1985.

The Final Compulsory Purchase Orders

In 1984 the Corporation issued the final Compulsory Purchase Orders (CPOs) which applied to all remaining land not in its the possession, and specifically named the following plots: 'Everest' and 'Thorngrove' on First Avenue; 'Shanklin' in Stack Avenue; 'The Elms', 'Iona', 'High Trees', 'Four Elms' on Hillcrest Avenue; 'Roseglen' on Fourth Avenue; 'Tree Tops' and 'Chookaberry' on Western Avenue; and 'Anna Lina' on Lower Dunton Road.[1]

In accordance with the South West Area Plan, the Dunton Hills Estate was earmarked as open space. The South West Area Open Space Management Plan explained that the site was designed 'to form an extensive tract of semi-natural vegetation', which would form 'a cushion between the town and countryside'. As well as providing 'excellent opportunities for informal recreation such as walking and riding', its plotland heritage and the Plotland Museum would be 'a valuable educational resource'.[2]

Mark McManus met a number of the local residents at the time the CPOs were issued. He tells us their reactions:

'High Trees' and 'Four Elms' stood on a large plot on the highest point of Hillcrest Avenue. At the time of the CPOs the former was still being used as a weekend home but the latter had been cleared of its furniture.

'High Trees' and 'Four Elms' in Hillcrest Avenue, 1984.

Mrs Joyner, the lady who looked after the buildings, was possessed of a quiet determination. She told me that her small shacks had suffered continual break-ins from teenagers, gypsies, even drug addicts, and that 'Four Elms' was the property of an elderly aunt who was considering selling it to the Corporation. This part of the plotlands between Hillcrest Avenue and Lower Dunton Road was earmarked to become a Country Park. Mrs Joyner was sympathetic to the idea of a Country Park but wanted to retain her plot. As she told me, her family had been a part of the area before Basildon New Town had even existed … and she later fought for her right to stay until the moment the fight was lost.

When I first noticed the shack 'Viewgrand', standing in a dominant Hillcrest Avenue position which proved the accuracy of its name, I found it curious that such a ramshackle and clearly derelict building should be standing in a cropped garden rather than a tangle of undergrowth. I discovered the reason when I met its owner Mr Stanley Body, a cousin of Mrs Joyner who came from 'High Trees', further along the same avenue. He had bought the plot from its previous owner quite recently, and his intention was to renovate the building and to live in it! To that end, he had applied to the Council for planning permission which had been granted. Mr Body then tidied up the garden and laid new foundations to stabilise 'Viewgrand', only to receive the shock of finding a CPO staked to his newly cleared plot. You can imagine his annoyance, to be given the go-ahead by one local authority only to be halted by another, especially as he had already invested time and money in his dream. Like his cousin, he vowed to fight the Corporation.

'Viewgrand' in Hillcrest Avenue, 1984.

'Iona' on Hillcrest Avenue was the immediate neighbour of 'Viewgrand'. Although it appeared to be well looked after, I never saw 'Iona' being used in the few months I knew it. The owner decided not to oppose the CPO and sold the property to the Corporation. Consequently, 'Iona' fell to the bulldozer in the same week as 'Glencrest' and 'Maple Leaf'.

'Everest' stood at the top of First Avenue, at its junction with Hillcrest Avenue. At one time, it had served as the local shop. At the time of the

'Glencrest' in
Glenwood Gardens,
1984.

CPOs it was occupied by Florence
and John Elliot, and protected by
a pair of very loud and territorial
German shepherd dogs. Although
they had lived there for thirty years
and were saddened by the prospect of
leaving, the Elliots approached their
CPO with pragmatism rather than
reproach. They were in their 70s and
living in an area that was becoming
increasingly isolated. Having watched
their neighbours drift away over the
preceding three decades, they realised
that it was time for them to also depart
for a more convenient environment.
Accordingly, they instructed their
solicitor to negotiate a settlement
with the Corporation and moved
away in the spring of 1985. Two conifer trees which once
stood next to 'Everest' could barely be seen behind its
hedgerow at the time; nowadays they tower above it.

As its name suggests, 'Glencrest' stood at the junction
of Glenwood Gardens and Crest Avenue. It was used as
a holiday home, although the Electoral Register revealed
that it was providing a residence for the Hinchcliff Family
in 1964. It was a sturdy structure with a beautifully
maintained garden, surrounded by a high and dense
hedgerow. Despite the care taken to maintain it, the
owners did not contest the CPOs and the house was
bulldozed in the summer of 1984, at the same time as
'Iona' and 'Maple Leaf'. The nameplates of all three were
salvaged and displayed in the Plotland Museum for over
two decades.

'Thorngrove' was one of the last plots to be used as a
full-time residence. Its resident, Charlie Thompson, was
a familiar figure, often to be seen shuffling along First
Avenue, long coat down to his knees, shoulders hunched,
a rolled-up cigarette clenched between his lips. He was
somewhat reclusive, little given to idle chatter, and the
only resident of Dunton Hills not to own a dog. Somehow,
Charlie managed to stay in his home after the trauma of
the CPOs. He died there in the autumn of 1992, and the
gnarled ruins of 'Thorngrove' can still be seen today in
the tangled undergrowth.

'Hawthorn', Hillcrest Avenue, was first a holiday
home, then a main home for the Burke Family who

'Hawthorn' in Hillcrest Avenue, 1984.

Site of 'Hawthorn' on Hillcrest Avenue, 2009.

held it from the 1930s until 1983. Following this, it was occupied by successive wardens of the Nature Reserve's Plotland Musuem until the construction of the Visitor Centre at the western end of Third Avenue. Despite falling from use, 'Hawthorn' survived until 1999. Its outline is clearly discernible today.

The 1984 Public Inquiry

The objections from many remaining plotlanders meant that a public inquiry was held in December 1984. Nick Street from the Planning Department had to prepare evidence for the inquiry, which was held in the Community Centre near the Triangle Shops in Langdon Hills High Road. He recalls the weather turned bitterly cold and the heating wasn't working. Several people left early, blaming the Corporation for the freezing conditions. Nick had to phone the housing department to get some heaters delivered for the afternoon. The inquiry lasted two days, with oral evidence presented by the objectors on the first day and a site visit to the plotlands on the second. Nick had to lend the Chairman a pair of wellies for the site visit as the lanes were so muddy!

Mark McManus gives us his eyewitness account of the meeting:

I 'absented' myself from college for a couple of days in order to attend. The chairman of the Inquiry, appointed by the powers at Whitehall, was one Cecil Hyams. The spokesman for the Corporation was a bespectacled, earnest man named Crawford Lindsay. I did not envy him his task. Behind his seat were rows of chairs occupied by angry plotlanders. He must have felt their eyes burning into his back.

And what an array of plotlanders were gathered in this small hall! Mrs Joyner was there with her cousin, Mr Body; the owner of the recently demolished 'Iona' attended as an observer; Mrs Royden, a Fourth Avenue plotlander; Mr Hollands; Mrs Bonnett who had once owned property in First Avenue and Lower Dunton Road; and Mr Mott of 'Mon Ami' in the Lower Dunton Road.

Crawford Lindsay gave a very long opening speech in which he laid out the plans that the Corporation had for the area, and the necessity of using CPOs to possess all the land before creating a country park. After his speech, many of the plotlanders stepped forward to have their say. One visitor, an ex-plotlander himself, actually supported the Corporation. He argued that to show favour to Dunton Hills would be unfair to the thousands of other families who had been forced to sell their homes as Basildon New Town grew.

Mrs Royden gave the most upsetting speech. She had owned a shack which was the last plot still in use in Fourth Avenue, and it had burned down only a few weeks previously. Her voice became very emotional as she talked of her wish to rebuild, and her frustration at the destruction of her holiday home so soon before she was due to speak in its defence.

Mr Mott was the angriest orator, and the most experienced, having spoken at the previous Inquiry in 1974. He accused the Corporation of deliberately waiting until the plots had become mostly abandoned before issuing the CPOs, in an attempt to save money as many of the landowners would not learn that their plots were under threat.

That day was the last time I saw the weekenders. Some months later, the decision had been made. The CPOs would go ahead, and the fight to protect the last private plots had been lost.

The subsequent years saw many changes. Basildon Development Corporation was succeeded by the Commission for New Towns, who sold the Estate to Essex Wildlife Trust. A Visitor Centre was built at the foot of Third Avenue. The abandoned plotland buildings continued to collapse, burn or be demolished. By the time the bulldozers arrived to lay the groundwork for the Great Berry Development, only one derelict remained

All that remains of the corner of Crest Avenue and Glenwood Gardens, 2010.

'Everest' on First
Avenue, 1984.

standing: 'St Jean' in Margaret Avenue, and even this
old house was in a skeletal state. The bulldozers, as they
flattened and crushed, swept away not only trees and
rubble but the physical remains of a lost way of life. The
last plotlander, old Charlie who lived in Second Avenue,
managed to stay (barricaded away) on his land until the
autumn of 2006, when he moved away due to ill-health.

As Mark showed above, accounts of the final days of the plots
on the Dunton Hills Estates provide a sad ending to the plotland
tale. Even 25 years on, Ken Royden, whose family owned a plot
in Fourth Avenue from the 1940s until the mid-1980s, still bitterly
remembers the wave of arson in the area:

In the last few months the bungalow was broken into
and most of the items stolen several times before they
burnt it out. They had two attempts. The first time
they broke a window and set light to the curtains but
it went out. A couple of weeks later they used petrol.
When it was burnt out by arson in them days you had to
rebuild immediately or apply for planning permission,
which gave you three years' grace to start work. Even
though it was arson the Council still refused us planning
permission. The repossession was completed a few
months after.

Mysterious fires were not confined to the 1980s. Carole Devlin
told us that even back in the 1960s her family's bungalow 'Jessica' in
Sylvan Road, Laindon, was burnt down while they were finalising

its compulsory purchase. However, the Dunton area suffered very badly from attacks in the final months.

The notes below are from records held at the Nature Reserve relating to the final days of 'Everest' on First Avenue. They paint a depressing picture. It is poignant to note that the 1984 CPO came into force on 30 April 1985 – the Elliots moved out on 29 April:

Monday 29 April 1985	Mr and Mrs Elliot moved out of 'Everest'.
30 April 1985	'Everest' broken into and fire started.
1 May 1985	Police called re: 'Everest' break-in.
15 May 1985	Fire at 'Anthelen' and 'Rosalie'.
21 May 1985	Windows taken from 'Everest'.
23 May 1985	'Everest' burnt down.

The piles of charred remains littering the Dunton site were sad funeral pyres for once-cherished buildings. Even in their often dilapidated states, they still represented their former owners' ambitions, hopes and efforts ...

Helen Anthony proudly surveying the view from 'Anthelen' on Fourth Avenue.

Chapter 17

Final Thoughts

Researching and writing this book has been a complete joy. Peter and I have spent many delightful hours talking to ex-plotlanders, corresponding with them via letter and email, and poring over their wonderful photographs. We have been struck by their enthusiasm and passion for their former plots, and their determination that the plotland way of life should not simply be allowed to disappear from memory. Such was the sense of community that many of them have kept in touch since they were children attending the local Dunton School in the 1940s, and hold regular reunions. Others act as volunteers in 'The Haven' plotland museum at the Langdon Nature Reserve. Those who owned a plotland property felt they were very privileged to have experienced this lifestyle, and this is probably one of the reasons why friendships have endured. Indeed, I still keep in contact with fellow plotlanders from my childhood.

Ironically, the Basildon plotland community was a victim of its own success. Hundreds of families may have enjoyed the benefits of 'the good life', but the local council could not ignore the fact that there were so many people living in 'substandard' housing. Health officials were also concerned that the lack of mains water and sewerage made for unsanitary living conditions. With minimal rates contributions, the authorities could not afford to make any improvements even where residents were asking for them. And so the axe had to fall.

Are the plotlands just a peculiar legacy of the past, a brief quirky period in history that, thanks to draconian planning legislation, can never be repeated again? Or are there lessons from the plotland experience that could serve us well in future? We believe there are. Clearly we cannot claim to be experts in any of these fields, but we offer our personal thoughts below.

We must bear in mind that we have been interacting with ex-plotlanders who have a positive view of the past. There may be many others who did not enjoy their experiences of plotland life – and therefore did not feel the same urge to contact us. Even for the most ardent fans, memories can sometimes cheat and the past

Peter's grandparents outside their self-built home, 'Vera-Joan'.

can seem rosier than it did at the time. However, many people hold firm beliefs that although they only had basic facilities and few material goods, the freedom and proximity to nature more than compensated for any hardships. As a child I thought my family was rich because we had our hut at Laindon and my summers were spent in the countryside. To me, the paraffin lamps and the Jeyes-filled toilet bucket in a shed seemed to be the trappings of wealth, not poverty. It therefore came as a complete shock to be told by my mum during an episode of 'Upstairs, Downstairs' that we were actually very poor and would definitely have been part of the 'downstairs' crew.

In the 1980s, a major academic study of the plotland pheno-menon established its significance in the progress of 'ordinary citizens' towards economic and personal empowerment.[1] Owning a little piece of land was the key. Much can be said for the personal satisfaction and pride that people experienced from designing, building and maintaining their own home on their own land. Many of these people would never have been able to afford to buy a house in the normal housing market, so would have spent their lives living in rented accommodation. The plotlands gave them a chance to control their own destiny and free themselves from landlords – at least for a short while.

Does the simple architecture of the plotlands still have some-thing to offer us for the future? In the United States there has been a growing interest in what is known as 'the small house movement'. A website for 'The Small House Society' offers advice to people who wish to construct their own diminutive dwellings. It notes there has been a dramatic increase in interest in downsizing property for a variety of reasons, such as: economic factors (it costs less to build, heat and maintain a smaller property); environmental factors (using fewer materials and sustainable timber is more environmentally friendly); and a desire to lead a simpler existence.[2] Who knows, perhaps a 21st-century version of plotland architecture might rise like a phoenix from the demolished and charred remains of the former plotland movement.

The plotland era also reminds us that people can live happily in a more sustainable way. Around the UK, living 'off-grid' without mains services is still a way of life for some people, particularly those who wish to make use of sustainable technology to power their homes. Faced with energy challenges in the future, more will have to be done to encourage people to take responsibility for supplying or managing their own energy needs. As any ex-plotlander will tell you, there's nothing quite like knowing that you only have enough paraffin to power one lamp to help you cut back on usage. Similarly, you certainly learn to be frugal with water if you have to keep lugging it backwards and forwards in a metal jug from a standpipe several hundred yards away.

Peter and I have lost count of the number of times people have recalled with pleasure the freedom they had as children to roam around the countryside, often alone – as Peter did in the 1950s and 1960s and I did in the 1970s. Normally people then add: 'You couldn't do that nowadays.' The Wildlife Trusts have recognised that many young people have lost this freedom to explore and connect with nature, and have been working hard to re-engage them. As a society we certainly cannot afford to become distanced from our natural environment, which sustains us in more ways than we often realise.[3]

The Anderson family and friends at 'Iris Villa', 1950s.

David Blaine shows how plotland children kept fit. 'Westholme', Sidney Road, late 1940s.

More than one person has spoken of the 'therapeutic' legacy of the plotlands, noting that there was a special atmosphere about the place which still lingers on the reserve today. Plotlanders were definitely very close to nature and the permanent residents would have been very aware of the passing of the seasons and the different challenges they brought. Most of the time was spent outside: tending flower gardens; growing their own fruit and vegetables; mowing unruly lawns; keeping overhanging bushes trimmed in the lanes; mending ruts in the roads and maintaining paths; playing games on home-made golf courses, badminton courts and the like; exploring; blackberry picking; or simply going for lengthy walks in the countryside. In the last decade, researchers from the University of Essex have been studying the benefits of 'green exercise' on both physical and mental health. They believe that: 'There is a synergistic benefit in adopting physical activities whilst at the same time being directly exposed to nature.'[4] These findings could have a significant effect on health care in the future.

Enjoying 'green exercise': the Andersons of 'Bonanza' in High View Avenue, 1969.

Whether or not we can learn lessons from the plotlands, we think it is important that they are not forgotten. Hopefully this book has helped to bring a few more of the little wooden huts and grassy lanes back to life again. And to everyone who took up a hammer or scythe – we salute you!

The sun sets over the plotlands – 'Coombe Cottage' and 'Wendover'.

References

ERO = Essex Records Office
BDC = Basildon Development Corporation

Chapter 1
1. Hardy and Ward, *Arcadia For All* (reprinted 2004)
2. 'The Truth About Bungalows' article on findaproperty.com (2003)
3. Minutes from BDC meeting of 8 March 1973, held at ERO
4. Cuttle Collection of newspaper cuttings from the *Essex Chronicle*, 23/1/1931, ERO
5. Reeve, *Basildon Memories*, p.25

Chapter 2
1. Age and Condition Surveys of the Laindon, Langdon Hills and Dunton area conducted in 1949-50. Held by ERO as part of the BDC archive.
2. Hardy and Ward, *op. cit.*, p.205
3. Basildon New Town Master Plan Technical Report 1951, p.11
4. 'Shack Clearance: A Preliminary View of the Problem', report to the BDC board meeting, 7 July 1950
5. Letter from Ministry of Town & Country Planning to BDC officer, 23/8/49. Correspondence held by ERO as part of BDC archive.
6. 'Shack Clearance' report, *op. cit.*
7. Young, *Down the Line* (2005), pp. 7 and 14

Chapter 3
1. 1970 South West Area Plan
2. Age and Condition Survey data held by ERO, *op. cit.* Detailed surveys of estate conducted 6/12/49-5/4/50.
3. McKay, *Plotland Memories* (2000)

Chapter 6
1. Age and Condition Survey data held by ERO, *op. cit.* Detailed surveys of estate conducted 12/12/49-28/12/49.
2. Hill, *Britain in Old Photographs: Basildon* (1999), p.13

3. Ross, *Basildon 1915-1986* (1986), p.5.
4. *Ibid.*, p.1
5. *Ibid.*, p.44
6. *Ibid.*, p.60
7. Dunton Parish Invasion Committee Household Survey, 1942, courtesy of David Richards

Chapter 8
1. Basildon Development Corporation Annual Report 1959, HMSO, p.47

Chapter 9
1. Age and Condition Survey held by ERO, *op. cit.* Detailed surveys of estate conducted 20/12/49-21/12/49
2. 1950 Register of Electors. Parliamentary Consituency: Billericay. Polling District: Langdon Hills.
3. Reeve, *op. cit.*, p. 26

Chapter 10
1. Age and Condition Survey held by ERO, *op. cit.* Detailed surveys of the estate conducted 9/12/49-18/1/50.

Chapter 12
1. Roger J.C. Thomas, *Prisoner of War Camps (1939-1948)*, English Heritage: Twentieth Century Military Recording Project, 2003
2. ERO: SEAX 'Unlocking Essex's Past', http://unlockingessex.essexcc.gov.uk/
3. ARP Incident Files, Billericay Area, 15/1/44-26/11/44, ERO
4. Hayes, *Plotland Album: The Story of the Dunton Hills Community* (1984), p.29
5. Neale, *Essex in History* (1997), p.157
6. Hansard: Sir John Anderson, the Lord President of the Council, House of Commons, 24 March 1942
7. David Richards, 'Lord Leatherland', http://www.charlesleatherland.info/
8. Minutes, Dunton Parish Invasion Committee (PIC), 6 March 1942, courtesy of David Richards
9. Minutes, Dunton PIC, 13 March 1942, courtesy of David Richards
10. Minutes, Laindon and District Central Invasion Committee, 25 June 1942, courtesy of David Richards
11. Charles Leatherland, personal papers, courtesy of David Richards
12. Dunton PIC Household Survey, 194, courtesy of David Richards
13. Minutes, Horndon-on-the-Hill Parish Invasion Committee, 17 March 1943, ERO

14. Communication: Billericay Urban District Council, Air Raid Precautions Department, 2 October 1942, courtesy of David Richards
15. Dunton School Log Book, 1931-45, ERO

Chapter 13
1. *Kelly's Directory*, 1922
2. Dunton School Log Book, 1931-45, ERO
3. Sheila Mountfort, and Ivy Titchen, *Portrait of Dunton the Lost Village* (1988)
4. Dunton School Log Book, 1932, ERO
5. *Ibid.*, July 1931
6. BDC 6th Annual Report in 'Reports of the Development Corporations', HMSO (1955)
7. Basildon History website http://www.basildon.com/history/
8. Ross, *Brink of Despair* (1986), p.20.
9. *Ibid.*, p.114
10. Hayes, *Plotland Album*, p.30.

Chapter 14
1. Lucas, *Basildon Birth of a City* (1986), p.1
2. Ross, *op. cit.*, p.66
3. *Ibid.*, p.67
4. *Ibid.*, p.71
5. BDC 1st Annual Report in 'Reports of the Development Corporations 31 March 1950', HMSO (1950), p.42
6. Minutes from BDC Board meeting, 16 March 1949
7. *Ibid.*
8. Minutes from BDC Board meeting, 22 July 1949
9. Minutes from BDC Board meeting, 26 October 1949
10. Master Plan for Basildon 1950, p.10
11. Minutes from BDC Board meeting, 8 December 1950
12. Minutes from BDC Board meeting, 14 September 1951
13. Minutes from BDC Board meeting, 9 November 1951
14. Minutes from BDC Board meetings, 23 May and 19 September 1955
15. BDC 2nd Annual Report in 'Reports of the Development Corporations 31 March 1951', HMSO (1951)
16. Minutes from BDC Board meeting, 7 July 1950
17. BDC 3rd Annual Report in 'Reports of the Development Corporations 31 March 1952', HMSO (1952), p.55
18. BDC 5th Annual Report in 'Reports of the Development Corporations 31 March 1954', HMSO (1951), p.51
19. BDC 6th Annual Report in 'Reports of the Development Corporations 31 March 1955', HMSO (1955), p.43
20. BDC 7th Annual Report in 'Reports of the Development Corporations 31 March 1956', HMSO (1956)
21. BDC 10th Annual Report in 'Reports of the Development

Corporations 31 March 1959', HMSO (1959), p.46
22. *Ibid.*, p.43
23. Chief Estates Officer's Report to BDC, November 1952
24. Ross, *op. cit.*, p.98
25. Letter from Noel Tweddell to J. Austin, 14 July 1950. Held by ERO as part of the BDC archive.
26. Letter from J. Austin to Noel Tweddell, 20 July 1950. Held by ERO as part of the BDC archive.
27. BDC 1st Annual Report, in 'Reports of the Development Corporations 31 March 1950', HMSO (1950)
28. J. Austin's survey of building operatives sent to Noel Tweddell in July 1950. Held by ERO as part of the BDC archive.
29. Colin Ward, 'The Basildon Story: Some Lessons from Shanty Town', *Royal Institute of British Architects Journal*, February 1974
30. Letter from Charles Boniface to Alma Hatt, 23 April 1964. Held by ERO as part of the BDC archive.
31. Letter from Paul Channon, June 1973. Held by ERO as part of the BDC archive.
32. Basildon History website http://www.basildon.com/history/

Chapter 15
1. Urban District of Basildon Official Guide, 1968.
2. Minutes from BDC Board meeting, 5 April 1973.
3. *Ibid.*
4. BDC 26th Annual Report in 'Reports of the Development Corporations 31 March 1975', HMSO 1975, p.35
5. Minutes from BDC Board meeting, 13 June 1974
6. Minutes from BDC Board meeting, 10 October 1974
7. BDC Annual Report in 'Reports of the Development Corporations 31 March 1975', HMSO 1975, p.34

Chapter 16
1. Compulsory Purchase Orders for Dunton Estate published on Basildon History website http://www.basildon.com/history/
2. South West Open Space Management Plan

Chapter 17
1. Hardy and Ward, *op. cit.*
2. Interview by Gregory Johnson on his website for the Small House Society, http://www.resourcesforlife.com/small-house-society
3. For further reading on reconnecting with nature see Jules Pretty, *The Earth Only Endures. On Reconnecting with Nature and Our Place in it* (2007), Earthscan, London
4. Pretty, Griffin, Sellens, Hine and Peacock (eds), 'Green Exercise – The Mental and Physical Health Benefits of Physical Activity', *Guide to a Healthy Planet* (2006)

Bibliography

Currie, I., Davison, M. and Ogley, B., *The Essex Weather Book* (1992), Froglets Publications, Kent

Hardy, Dennis and Ward, Colin, *Arcadia For All. The Legacy of a Makeshift Landscape* (reprinted 2004), Five Leaves Publications, Nottingham

Hayes, Pat, *Plotland Album: The Story of the Dunton Hills Community* (1984), Basildon Development Corporation, Basildon

Hill, Marion, *A Century of Basildon* (2000), Sutton, Stroud

Hill, Marion, *Britain in Old Photographs: Basildon* (1999), Sutton, Stroud

Lucas, Peter, *Basildon* (1991), Phillimore, Chichester

Lucas, Peter, *Basildon: Birth of a City* (1986), Basildon Printing Co., Wickford

Lyons, Mary, *The Story of the Jaywick Sands Estate* (2005), Phillimore, Chichester

McKay, Karen, *Plotland Memories* (2000), Essex Wildlife Trust, Langdon Reserve, Basildon

Neale, Kenneth, *Essex in History* (1997), Phillimore, Chichester

Payne, Jessie, *Basildon: A Pictorial History* (1981), Phillimore, Chichester

Pretty, Jules, *The Earth Only Endures. On Reconnecting with Nature and Our Place in it* (2007), Earthscan, London

Pretty, J., Sellens, M., South, N. and Wilson, M. (eds), *Guide to a Healthy Planet* (2006), University of Essex, Colchester

Reeve, Jim, *Basildon Memories* (2006), Tempus, Stroud

Rosen, Nick, *How to Live Off-Grid. Journeys Outside the System* (2007), Transworld, London

Ross, George, *Basildon 1915-1986 From Country Life to the Brink of Despair when the Bulldozers Take Over* (1986), Basildon Printing Co., Wickford

Searle, Muriel, *Down the Line to Southend* (1984), Baton Press, Tunbridge Wells

Walker, Deanna, *Basildon Plotlands: The Londoners' Rural Retreat* (2001), Phillimore, Chichester

Young, Allan, *Down the Line: Memories of the Dunton Bungalow Estate 1935-1953* (2005), self-published

Websites

See Peter Jackson's Dunton Plotland website for additional photographs from ex-plotlanders:
http://www.roselake.co.uk/

Basildon History Online:
http://www.basildon.com/history/home.html

ERO – SEAX 'Unlocking Essex's Past':
http://unlockingessex.essexcc.gov.uk/

Essex Wildlife Trust, 'The Langdon Reserve':
http://www.essexwt.org.uk/

Richards, David, 'Charles Leatherland':
http://www.charlesleatherland.info/

Wallace Jackson's squadron in the Second World War:
http://www.70squadron.roselake.co.uk/index.htm

Index of Plotlands and Lanes

Please note that not all plots mentioned in passing in this book are listed in the index. References to illustrations are given **in bold**.